# RETHINKING
# REFERENCE

RETHINKING
REFERENCE

THE
REFERENCE
LIBRARIAN'S
PRACTICAL
GUIDE
FOR
SURVIVING
CONSTANT
CHANGE

ELIZABETH
THOMSEN

D1532362

## Neal-Schuman Publishers, Inc.

New York                    London

**Library of Congress Cataloging-in-Publication Data**

Thomsen, Elizabeth.
  Rethinking reference: the reference librarian's practical guide for surviving constant change / Elizabeth Thomsen.
    p. cm.
  Includes biographical references (p.) and index.
  ISBN 1-55570-364-X
  1. Reference services (Libraries)--United States. I. Title.

Z711.T489 1999
025.5'2 21--dc21                           99-043740

Published by Neal-Schuman Publishers, Inc.
100 Varick Street
New York, NY 10013
Copyright © 1999 by Elizabeth Thomsen

Printed and bound in the United States of America.

ISBN 1–55570–364–X

# Table of Contents

# List of Figures

# Preface

Technology has altered almost all aspects of our lives, particularly our work life. Perhaps more than any other profession, technology has succeeded in transforming the way librarians interact with users, the ways they collect information, and even the way they think about what collections of information look like. As the primary link between users and library services, reference librarians are particularly affected by rapid and radical changes in the ways information is packaged and the ways people access it. In order to meet the challenges that the information age brings with it, reference librarians must continually adapt to changing user expectation and new tools.

*Rethinking Reference: The Reference Librarian's Practical Guide for Surviving Constant Change* has three purposes. First, it attempts to provide a perspective for looking at how traditional reference service "fits" in with new trends and issues. Secondly, it documents the myriad ways in which day-to-day library services are being transformed by changes in technology, culture, and staffing. Finally, it offers guidance and advice for both evolving reference services to adapt to these changes (so we can all survive) and for communicating the value of those services to administrators and funders.

*Rethinking Reference: The Reference Librarian's Practical Guide for Surviving Constant Change* is intended to be a practical resource for reference librarians in all sizes and types of libraries and for both seasoned and beginning reference librarians. Students in library and information studies (LIS) programs may also find this a "real world" introduction to the complexities of contemporary reference work. The author particularly hopes readers working in libraries will find portions of this text helpful to give to trustees and other funding authorities to help them understand how librarians must deal with the current enthusiasm for electronic information.

The volume is arranged in nine chapters which address different aspects of reference work. Each chapter uses sidebars and tables which present strategies for success, observations of developing trends, tips on providing services, and Web sites that will make keeping current easier.

Chapter 1, "Reference: The Nature of the Business," is a brief history of the role of the reference librarian over the last century. It stresses the need to work toward a constantly evolving model of reference to continue serving users' needs.

Chapter 2, "The Changing Role of the Reference Librarian," discusses the function and characteristics of a reference librarian and how the profession has changed dramatically with the advent of electronic resources. It also addresses changes in staff relationships, in collection development issues, and budget issues, showing a shift in emphasis from acquisition to access.

Chapter 3, "Communication Skills," discusses the nature of effective communication, the particular communication challenges of reference work, the reference interview, and the implications of the Americans with Disabilities Act (ADA) for reference librarians. Because the reference process is presented as a type of interaction rather than a series of tasks or activities, communication skills are crucial.

Chapter 4, "Resources," starts with a short history of reference collections followed by the use and evaluation of reference resources in the electronic age, from traditional reference books to competition from commercial sources in filling information needs.

Chapter 5, "Time and Space," looks at the layout, use, and staffing of the reference area and addresses the critical question, "How does reference happen?"

Chapter 6, "Questions, In and Out," looks at questions from all angles: the reasons people have questions, how they ask questions, the types of questions they have, tricky and difficult questions, directory questions, contest questions, homework questions, policies on questions, and using the Web to answer questions.

Chapter 7, "Reference Librarians as Trainers and Pathfinders," points out that librarians need training to keep up with the many different formats and points of view, and in turn, they need to train the users. Training methods are included in the discussion.

Chapter 8, "Statistics Can Help Ensure Quality," examines the caveats of measuring service with statistics and suggests methods for developing a plan for collecting and interpreting statistics to ensure quality service.

Chapter 9, "World Wide Web: Challenges and Opportunities," describes the Web in the context of reference services: what it has to offer; how it differs from other forms of reference; how it affects reference services (for example, policies, equipment, etc.), how library Web pages can contribute to high quality reference service.

Before, during, and after (if there will ever be an "after") the information revolution, the essence of good reference work has, is, and always will be a knowledgeable librarian providing personal service. Whether the service is provided on the phone, in person, or over the Internet, reference librarians are the ultimate generalists—essential links in connecting people with any information in any subject area. *Rethinking Reference: The Reference Librarian's Practical Guide for Surviving Constant Change* will serve as a useful guide to adapt to technological changes without losing the personal aspect of reference service.

# Acknowledgments

Much of what I know about reference I learned from conversations with other librarians. Some of the most helpful of these conversations took place not in individual libraries or at conferences, but in the e-mail groups. STUMPERS (*www.cuis.edu/~stumpers/*) is a fascinating, ongoing experiment in group reference. PUBLIB (*http://sunsite.berkeley. edu/publib/*) often touches on reference and general public service issues.

But the premier e-mail group for reference librarians is LIBREF-L (*listserv.kent.edu/archives/libref-l.html*). Under the excellent management of several members of the Reference Services Team of Kent State University, LIBREF-L always offers interesting and thought-provoking discussions of both practical and philosophical reference matters. The searchable archives of this site are very useful for finding past discussions, and the list is also gatewayed to USENET as *bit.listserv.libref-l*, searchable through Deja (*www.deja.com.*) I have quoted extensively from LIBREF-L discussions in this book, and would encourage people interested in a particular topic to go to the archives and read more.

I'd like to thank Mary Ellen Stasek of the Technology Center of Lakewood (Ohio) Public Library, for sharing her ideas and boundless enthusiasm on working with schools and other community groups and for permission to reprint screens from the Technology Center of the Lakewood Public Library. You'll find quotations from e-mail messages I received from Mary Ellen and examples of screens from some of their projects in Chapter 7, but I encourage you to visit the library's Web site at *www.lkwdpl.org/* to see much more.

I'd also like to thank Joanne Kares and the reference staff of the Morris County (N.J.) Public Library. The library's Web-based reference pathfinders, prepared by Sara Weissman, Donna Burkey, and other members of the staff, are all excellent. Eureka!, (*www.gti.net/mocolib1/monthly. html*) the Library's monthly reference alert service edited by Lynne Olver, is exceptional.

Special thanks to the North Suburban Library System, especially System Director Sarah Ann Long and Assistant Director, Membership and Marketing, Mary Witt, for permission to include material from their Reference Librarians Association's excellent "Reference Evaluation Project." Their reference policy is reproduced in Appendix A in its entirety, and is a model that can benefit many other libraries.

Interesting insights on reference and library services in general, from both administrative and public service perspectives, came from my personal advisory board of distinguished librarians: Patrick J. Cloherty, Jr., Michael Colford, Laurie Formichella, Ronald A. Gagnon, Sharon Gilley, Jeffrey Klapes, Lori Stalteri, and Charlotte Thompson. Margaret Thomsen, Kristin Thomsen, and Jeanne Denning always provide interesting insights from the patron's perspective.

I'd like to thank the following librarians for permission to use quotations from LIBREF messages: Alicia Barraqué Ellison, Jeffrey A. Beck, Anne Berwind, Jay Evatt, Kelli Perkins, Catherine P. Cox, Robert Boyce, Susan E. Thomas, Laura K. Brendon, Robert Lee Hadden, Marge Fauver, and Paul Nelson.

I'd also like to thank R. David Lankes for permission to use quotations and a screen image from the Virtual Reference Desk and the following for permission to use screen images from their sites: Gary Price for Price's List of Lists and Direct Search; Richard Tchen for Ask Dr. Math; Franklin Smiles for the Jewish Torah Audio Site; Walter F. Nickeson for the Library Support Staff Resource Center; Marylaine Block for BIOTN, the Best Information on the Net; David S. Carter for the Internet Public Library; Stephen Lim for NeWo News Resource page; the Perry-Castañeda Library of the University of Texas at Austin for the PCL Map Collection; and AltaVista for the AltaVista Translation Assistant (the AltaVista Logo and Search Engine Content are copyright and trademarks of AltaVista Company; used with permission).

I'd also like to thank the following for permission to use quotations:

Sharon M. West and Steven L. Smith for permission to quote from their presentation at the 1995 CAUSE Conference, "Library and Computing Merger: Clash of the Titans or Golden Opportunity?"

Sage Publications, 2455 Teller Rd., Thousand Oaks, CA 91320 for permission to quote from David R. Majka's article "Developing an Electronic Tickler File for Reference Collection Management." *Library Software Review* 14, no.

3: 146–153. Used with permission of Sage Publications, Inc.

Information Today, Inc. (143 Old Marlton Pike, Medford, NJ 08055-8750, *www.infotoday.inc.*) for permission to use quotations from Maurice York's article "Value-Added Reference Service: the North Carolina Periodicals Index" from *Computers in Libraries*; and Irene E. McDermott's article "Virtual Reference for a Real Public," from *Searcher*.

Conference Board, Inc. (845 Third Avenue, New York, NY 10022) for permission to use quotations from Keith E. Ferrazzi and Ernest Riddle from an article by A.J. Vogt published in *Across the Board*.

# Chapter 1

# Reference: The Nature of the Business

As we move into the 21st century, librarianship is being transformed in response to great changes in society as well as to our own evolving sense of direction for the profession. Reference librarians, always on the front lines of the profession, connecting library patrons and library services, are especially sensitive to these changes and to the confusion and stress that change can bring. To understand the role of reference librarians, it might be useful to look back to the end of the last century, also a time of great change, and the period that in many senses defined our libraries and our roles within them.

## IN THE BEGINNING: 1875–1900

The last quarter of the 19th century was a time of growth and change in America. The wounds of the Civil War were healing, and the railroad was opening up the West. New technologies, like the telephone and telegraph systems, had dramatically changed communications in the nation and were transforming business and journalism. The country's economy was shifting from an agricultural to an industrial base. Urbanization and immigration were concentrating the population in the burgeoning cities.

American idealism was running high in the 1870s and 1880s, and perhaps the dominant theme was that of opportunity. Farm boys flocked to the city hoping to strike it rich through hard work and pluck. Young women came as well, to work in domestic service or in factories, or to enter the emerging professional fields of education, nursing, social work, journalism, and librarianship.

Immigrants flocked to our shores, to discover that even if the streets were not paved with gold, there was opportunity here to work hard, save money, and become a success. The novels of Horatio Alger were popular because they expressed the optimism of the time. Education was valued as the key to success, and night schools and settlement houses were established to bring learning to the masses.

It was during this time period, 1875–1900, that both the institution of the public library and the profession of librarianship were truly born. The American Library Association and *Library Journal* were both founded in 1876. The endlessly enthusiastic and shamelessly self-promoting Melvil Dewey was in his prime. The great libraries of New York, Boston, Philadelphia, and San Francisco were built, and Scottish industrialist and philanthropist Andrew Carnegie was transforming small-town America, one library at a time. Carnegie's motivation, in his own words, was "to help those who will help themselves, to provide part of the means by which those who desire to improve may do so; to give those who desire to rise the aids by which they may rise . . . " (*Library Journal*, 1996).

The public library was seen as the people's university, steeped in a traditional sense of scholarly values, but open to all. The early literature on librarianship reflects this evangelist zeal, this desire to bring culture and enlightenment to the masses, the desire to educate and improve, the belief in enlightenment through literature, the ideal of the library as " . . . a means for enriching, beautifying and making fruitful the barren places in human life" (Eastman, 1897, p. 80).

It was in this context that the concept of reference librarianship began to develop. The most influential voice in this area was Samuel Swett Green of the Worcester Free Public Library in Massachusetts, one of the founders of *Library Journal*. In an 1876 article, "Personal Relations Between Librarians and Readers," Green outlined the major democratic principle of the profession:

> When scholars and persons of high social position come to a library, they have confidence enough, in regard to the cordiality of their reception, to make known their wishes without timidity or reserve. Modest men in the humbler walks of life, and well-trained boys and girls, need encouragement before they become ready to say freely what they want (Green, 1876).

Green's language has a quaintness when we read it today, and yet he manages to convey the essence of much modern customer service training:

A hearty reception by a sympathizing friend, and the recognition of some one at hand who will listen to inquiries, even although he may consider them unimportant, make it easy for such persons to ask questions, and put them at once on a home footing (Green, 1876).

Professional reference services developed from these beginnings, and through the years, the language has evolved but the major issues haven't changed much. Reference services developed according to the spirit of the time, and in response to the austere, classical, closed-stack design of public and academic libraries of the time. The helpful instruction of the librarian was needed to find information in such a library, especially for the humble, nonscholarly folk. And despite the differences in language, Green and other writers of the time touch on many of the basic issues that libraries still deal with. For example, Green has advice on proactive customer service:

A librarian should be as unwilling to allow an inquirer to leave the library with his question unanswered as a shop-keeper is to have a customer go out of his store without making a purchase.

He also offers advice on patron privacy:

Respect reticence. If you approach a reader with the purpose of aiding him, and find him unwilling to admit you to his confidence, regard his wishes and allow him to make investigations by himself.

Finally, Green touches on the neverending debate in reference between service and instruction:

> Be careful not to make inquirers dependent. Give them as much assistance as they need, but try at the same time to teach them to rely upon themselves and become independent (Green, 1876).

Throughout the 20th century, these same few basic issues continually resurface in the development of reference services in public, academic, and special libraries. How do we form a relationship with our patrons, so that we can understand their needs and find them the information they need, without making them feel uncomfortable and without violating their privacy? How do we balance between service (finding the answer for the patron) and instruction (teaching patrons how to find their own answers)?

The last quarter of the 19th century also established librarianship as a distinct profession, tied to a specific academic degree. As the library staff members in most direct contact with members of the community, this recognition of the profession was particularly important to reference librarians. And yet, despite the fact that the profession was defined and established over 100 years ago, issues of professional status and image continue to haunt us. Whether we are working on establishing and maintaining faculty status in the academic environment, dealing with the role of professionals and paraprofessionals at the reference desk, or expressing concern over the disappearance of "the L-word" from professional degree programs, the basic issues of identity and respect for our profession are still real and difficult issues.

## A CENTURY LATER: 1975–2000

The last quarter of the 20th century has seen an economic and social revolution that is as profound in its effect as the Industrial Revolution. Information has replaced industrialism, just as industrialism had replaced agriculture, and in each case these economic changes had profound social implications.

Computers began moving into businesses around 1950, but they didn't make much of an impact on most individuals until 1975, when Apple introduced the first small, personal computers (PCs) aimed at the home user. By the 1980s, desktop computers, used primarily for word processing, database, and spreadsheet applications, were everywhere—in offices, homes, and libraries.

The real revolution came in the 1990s, however, with the explosive development of the World Wide Web. The spread of the Web was helped along by a few other developments. Desktop computers became much faster and more powerful while also becoming much less expensive. Laptop, notebook, and now palmtop computers allowed people to be active and online even when they were away from their desktops—a real boon in a decade that also saw the globalization of many businesses and an increase in business travel. For the stay-at-home crowd, WebTV makes it possible for people to be on the Web without owning a computer at all. For those without access at home, cybercafes and commercial copy shops offer access—along with most libraries, of course. Internet Service Providers, or ISPs, are now everywhere, and business is competitive. In addition to the "traditional" independent

ISPs, there are giants like America Online and alternative services from telephone and cable companies.

Another development that has greatly fueled the growth and influence of the World Wide Web is the introduction of free personal accounts for various services. This trend began with HotMail, the first service to offer free, advertising-supported e-mail accounts. HotMail was so successful that now hundreds of sites, from major portals like Yahoo to special-interest sites like the Discovery Channel and Catholic Online, offer free e-mail accounts. Sites supported by advertising offer free e-mail because it's a "sticky application," meaning that you'll be back day after day, checking your e-mail and also reading those ads. Deja.com, which began as a searchable archive service for USENET, now offers personal accounts for participating in USENET newsgroups. GeoCities, Tripod, and several other sites offer free Web site services. Yahoo, Delphi, and other sites offer the ability to set up "clubs" with open or restricted chat sessions, message boards, and the like.

All of these free services mean that anyone can participate in a variety of activities once he or she has access to a connected workstation. Furthermore, some services offer a free PC to those who meet certain criteria or agree to some conditions. More than one ISP already offers a free PC in exchange for a commitment of three years as a customer, and one online vendor offers a free PC for a commitment to spend at least $100 a month through their service.

## THE ECONOMICS OF THE INDUSTRIAL AGE AND THE INFORMATION AGE

Libraries are not only dealing with the great social changes of the Information Age and the World Wide Web, but also with some fundamental economic changes that affect libraries very directly.

In the industrial economy, machines were harnessed to manufacture goods, and workers became concentrated in urban areas to work in manufacturing. The industrial economy is based on economies of scale. Concentration of resources, including raw material, transportation, and a skilled workforce, enable big factories to build goods at a lower unit cost than small ones.

This model of concentrated resources and economies of scale extended to many areas of society beyond manufacturing. Large cities were able to support cultural resources, such as museums and symphony orchestras, because of the economies of scale in terms of potential audiences and donors. Higher education has also traditionally been conducted on a concentrated, economy of scale model in which hundreds (or thousands) of students are brought together to a single location, to be "processed" through a concentration of resources, including faculty, libraries, classrooms, and laboratories.

The great public libraries, established toward the end of the 19th century and growing through the 20th, are also based on the model of concentration of resources. Libraries were developed primarily for their collections, which were far more extensive than any individual could possibly own. Circulating collections were generally more extensive in size and scope than readers could find at

bookstores, and the ability to borrow, rather than purchase, books encouraged people to read far more extensively than they could have otherwise afforded.

Traditional reference collections also developed on the
principle of economies of scale. Most families could afford
some basic reference books, like a dictionary or almanac,
and some could afford an atlas and even a set of encyclopedias. Beyond these general sources, however, there are
many expensive and specialized reference works that very
few families could afford. Indeed, most of the works in
the traditional reference collection are not things that anyone would want to own, since they exist not to be read
but to be consulted occasionally as needed. Reference collections are cooperative ventures, where books that nobody
wants to own, but everyone potentially might need occasionally, are purchased and housed for the shared use of
the community. And, thanks to economies of scale, the
larger the community, generally speaking, the better the
collection.

In the postindustrial society, however, more of us are
involved in moving information around than in manufacturing goods, and, with the rapid growth of the Internet
in the last decade, we are seeing profound economic and
social changes. The old economic principles of concentration of resources and economies of scale no longer apply.

Information products are different from furniture or au-
tomobiles. It costs a lot to design a new automobile, but
it also costs a lot, in both resources and labor, to manufacture each individual vehicle. With information products,
most of the investment is in the design of the work: the
research, writing, and editorial work. The individual
units—for example, a set of encyclopedias, a book, or a

newspaper—are relatively inexpensive to produce and distribute. In the print world, the economies of scale exist not on the manufacturing side, but on the consumer side. A book needs to be priced so that the expected number of copies to be sold will recoup the initial investment plus a reasonable profit. This is why nonfiction generally costs more than fiction; why specialized books cost so much more than general interest ones, and why reference works and academic journals, with a potential buyership limited primarily to libraries, are traditionally extremely expensive.

Electronic publishing, however, does not follow the economic principles of traditional publishing. In the electronic world, information is expensive to produce but extremely inexpensive to reproduce. Each electronic copy is a perfect copy of the original, and costs the producer nothing, or nearly so. As long as the information exists on a reasonably robust Web server, on a reasonably robust network, an electronic journal or other resource can be reproduced endlessly in response to requests from different places.

To recoup the investment costs for the production of information, new models of electronic publishing are developing. Following the broadcast model of radio and television, some sites are supported by advertising. The information is free, but advertisers pay to get a share of the viewer's attention. Other sites charge for information on a pay-as-you-go basis. Many newspapers, for example, allow you to search their archives for free, but charge a few dollars to show you the full text of an article. Some sites are considered loss leaders by a parent institution; the electronic resources may not directly bring in any revenue, but they may increase brand recognition or loyalty to the primary business. Many television network sites fall into this category. Some electronic resources are supported by a membership fee. For example, you can search a variety of genealogical databases at Ancestry.com (*www.ancestry. com*), but to retrieve articles from many of the databases, you need to pay and become a member.

## DISINTERMEDIATION

The World Wide Web has greatly accelerated the process of disintermediation—otherwise known as eliminating the middleman. Disintermediation predated the Internet—consider how supermarkets disintermediated the grocer, who used to wait individually on customers and measure and weigh their purchases. ATMs disintermediated bank tellers from a large percentage of basic transactions. The World Wide Web, bringing a vast array of resources into homes and offices everywhere, is having a profound effect in many fields, and many occupations are feeling both the pinch and the promise of disintermediation.

Travel agents, for example, have served as intermediaries between travelers and the information needed to plan a trip, including complicated, proprietary airlines databases. Now anyone can access travel information and easily book his or her own flights, make hotel reservations, and consult maps and other travel information over the World Wide Web. Having just been disintermediated from a basic level of service, travel agencies are looking for new ways to provide added value and differentiate themselves in the marketplace.

Bankers and brokers are also feeling the effects of

disintermediation. Not only can consumers perform many transactions directly that they would formerly have needed to do through an intermediary, but in a networked world, location is no longer much of a factor. Consumers are free to shop for the best deal on a mortgage, for example, from any online financial institution, no matter where it is located, since all transactions can be done online.

In fact, some financial businesses are not really located anywhere, in the sense of having an office that you could visit. Thus as more and more people do their banking online and through ATMs, banks are finding that newcomer businesses, not encumbered by a large investment in branch offices and tellers, are often difficult to compete with.

Online shopping of all kinds is increasing exponentially, and is beginning to have an impact on the retail business. When a long-established independent bookstore in California's Silicon Valley went out of business recently, newspaper accounts attributed the demise of the business at least in part to the popularity of online bookseller Amazon.com.

### New Challenges

Reference librarians today are responding to changing circumstances, one of the most important of which is the blurring of distinctions between the roles of public and academic libraries. Not so long ago, college students were primarily young people, ages 18 to 22, who entered their full-time college studies directly from high school, and who lived on or near campus and used their college library almost exclusively for academic support. Now, college students may be 18 or 80 years old, may be taking courses full time or part time, and in any number of creative evening, weekend, or summer arrangements. They may live on campus, commute to campus, or be enrolled in distance education programs where the whole concept of campus becomes an analogy as much as a reality.

These changes affect both public and academic libraries. Public libraries now find that they are serving as the de facto academic library for many college students and for adults pursuing various educational options of many different kinds. Many public libraries now offer examination proctoring, formally or informally, for academic programs. Students participating in distance education programs of various kinds may also use public library Internet workstations. Sometimes this use involves uploading papers from diskette to the college server, or e-mailing them to an instructor, or participating in scheduled class chat sessions.

Academic libraries, at the same time, are dealing with students with a wide variety of backgrounds, circumstances, and experiences. New students may not have done library research for 20 years, and they may need much more orientation on full-text periodical databases and World Wide Web resources than the average new high school graduate.

These nontraditional students, however, seldom live on campus; they often have complex work and family commitments beyond their schoolwork, and they may be much less available for library tours and bibliographic instruction. If the academic library only provides professional reference services during daytime hours, the part-time students, who may only be able to come to the library during late evening hours, may be placed at a significant academic disadvantage.

Older students, individually and through programs like ElderHostel, have made academic libraries more aware of the need for large-print material, and students with young children have brought some new challenges to the academic library environment. Academic librarians are now dealing with policies on unattended children in the library, and some provide children's collections and services to help support these students with families.

## LIBRARIES OR COMPUTER CENTERS?

As libraries have added full, graphical Internet access to library workstations, librarians have run into a host of complex new issues. Librarians and members of the public approach library Internet access from opposite directions. Librarians are working from their traditional role and services, and we view Internet access as another way to provide the same research and information services that we have always provided. And, indeed, for patrons who come to the library to do research for a school paper or personal project, or for the person trying to track down some obscure fact, the World Wide Web can often provide just the information they need.

Library patrons, however, often have a different view. They are not necessarily researching a school paper or tracking down an obscure fact. They may not be traditional library users or traditional reference patrons at all. But they do know about the World Wide Web, and they are looking for access. They want access because they want to do the things that most people do with World Wide Web access: use e-mail, participate in discussion groups of various types, buy books and CDs and all sorts of other products online, make travel reservations, participate in online auctions, apply for a mortgage, renew their automobile registration, and generally participate in all aspects of the online world, many of which are beyond the scope of traditional library services.

The public Internet access offered by libraries has considerable competition—cybercafes; printing and business service centers offering PC use, including Internet access, by the hour; and pay Internet kiosks, which are springing up like pay phones in such public places as airports and malls. When people hear that a library offers public Internet access, they come to those workstations with a certain set of expectations. They know what they *can* do, and are unhappy when we do not permit the use of certain applications, such as e-mail or chat. As more and more people have experience with the Internet and have definite ideas about what they want to do on public workstations, reference librarians are spending as much time discussing the propriety of things like e-mail, chat, and games as they are discussing the pornography issues and the lack of satisfactory, widely accepted solutions.

Academic and public libraries face the same issues about the use of chat, e-mail, and games, but sometimes academic libraries try to restrict library workstations to academic and not recreational uses. Such restrictions, however, are exceedingly difficult and time-consuming to enforce. If you disallow access to e-mail, are you placing an unreasonable restriction on students who may receive course-related e-mail from the faculty, or who may be using e-mail to work with other students on group projects, or who may be waiting for a response to an e-mailed reference question? If library workstations offer restricted Internet access, while, on the other hand computer labs on campus offer unrestricted Internet access (including access to library databases), who would choose to work in the library?

As we struggle with these issues, we also find that even more complex problems arise. As more and more people are using computers at home and work, they may come to the library for a variety of tasks probably more suitable for a computer center. They want to go to a vendor's Web site to download printer drivers to a diskette to load on their home computer. They expect the library to provide the use of a scanner just as they want use of a photocopy machine. They bring diskettes of photographs straight from the drugstore's developing service and want to send them by e-mail to their friends or add them to a free Web site they are maintaining on GeoCities, or they want to download pictures from an e-mail message so they can edit them using a graphics program they have on their PC at home.

As the expectations of our library users increase, it becomes increasingly difficult to manage library workstations. Every effort to control resources seems to end up causing unforeseen problems for some groups of users. If we offer access to everything on every workstation, we have users who are frustrated because they can't access the library catalog without getting into a queue and reserving a workstation, a process that may take hours. If we segment access to different resources on different machines, we frustrate the user who wants to do a few different, related tasks—find an article on the Web and an article from the library's full-text periodicals database, e-mail them both to friends, and then cut and paste some quotes from one into a paper he or she is writing on the library's word processing program. A session like this could involve getting in queues for up to four different machines, and possibly discovering that some tasks couldn't be accomplished at all depending on how machines are set up, and whether or not the library allows patrons to use diskettes.

All of this is complex and frustrating for both patrons, whose expectations sometimes are not met, and for librarians, who are spending an increasing amount of time managing computer resources in ways that have little to do with reference. It's also complex and confusing for library administrators, and for the trustees of public libraries and college administrators overseeing academic libraries. How much money should be committed to adding, upgrading, and replacing computer workstations, printers, and networks? And where should that money come from—the materials budget, the staffing budget? Librarians would of course say that cuts in neither budget are acceptable, but money, unfortunately, must come from somewhere.

## REFERENCE SERVICE: TRADITIONAL AND PROACTIVE

Reference service, almost by definition, has a passive, reactive quality. (*Responsive* might be a more accurate, and certainly more flattering, term.) Patrons refer their questions to us, and we refer them to books, or refer to books ourselves to find the answers. And, traditionally, it's those books that are the authority, not us. We are trained always to quote the source, as part of our answer, and never to rely on our own memory, give our own opinion, or offer our own interpretation of any information that we provide. Our professionalism lies in selecting the best sources, both to add to the library's collection and to answer a particular question, but there is always a line that we do not cross. It's up to our patrons, and not us, to judge information and make decisions for themselves.

But firefighters and doctors and many other professionals have changed their focus in recent years, moving more into anticipatory and preventive services. Fire departments perform inspections and conduct educational campaigns to reduce the number of fires. Doctors and other health-care workers promote health and fitness. Reference librarians are also looking for better ways to serve the needs of our communities through proactive services.

Proactive service means something more than active service. Libraries can be very active, answering the same questions over and over, or they can be proactive and find ways to answer those questions before they are asked, before they even become questions. Proactive service can be accomplished in many ways, large and small. It's proactive service to approach a patron and offer help, rather than waiting for him to come to the reference desk and ask a question. It's proactive to give a patron your full attention and make sure that you understand her information need rather than just giving her a superficial answer to her opening question. It's proactive to teach classes and design training material on the effective use of electronic resources. And it's proactive to keep in contact with leaders in your organization or community, and to keep them informed about new information sources and services of interest to them.

Libraries are facing some of the same challenges as other businesses and institutions. For example, banks have a number of similarities with libraries. Banks and libraries both help people manage a valuable commodity: banks manage money and libraries manage information. Both services tend to have users who make frequent, basic transactions (deposits and withdrawals, checkins and checkouts), with occasional needs for a much higher level of service. A bank's customer needs time and attention to arrange for a mortgage, for example, and a library's customer needs the same kind of personal service for reference encounters.

One trend affecting both banks and libraries is the rising expectations of our clientele. People are busy these days, and they are no longer willing to accept old ways of doing business. Neil Levin writes:

> Bankers increasingly are recognizing that the banking industry is forever changed . . . and so are desperately trying to find ways to get the customers' attention and provide the ability to serve from wherever the customer chooses to be (Levin in Kay, 1997).

The same is true of librarians, whose customers are also unwilling to be limited to reference service at the library during certain hours. People want reference service by phone, fax, and e-mail. They want access to the online catalog at midnight and they want to be able to place their own reserves, requests, and renewals.

Articles about banking and businesses frequently use the phrase "multiple robust delivery channels." Libraries are also moving in this direction. "Multiple delivery channels" means many different ways are available for the customer to access the services of the institution, including walk-in service, phone, fax, and remote online access. "Robust" means that those delivery channels are reliable, have sufficient capacity to support the maximum predictable number of simultaneous users, and are easy to access. It's no good to offer remote online access if the system is frequently down and it's no good to offer phone service if people frequently encounter busy signals or lengthy periods of time on hold.

Ernest Riddle of Ryder International says, "As the business becomes more unpredictable, you need to be more flexible so that you can be there when the customer wants something." (Riddle, in Vogl, 1997). Libraries also need to be accessible when the customer wants something. Libraries are not the only source of information in our customers' lives; in an "information society," we have competition on all sides. People have access to bright and lively superstores, with a dazzling array of books, comfortable chairs, and cappuccino. They have hundreds of television stations via cable or satellite, including specialized networks like CNN, the Discovery Channel, and Food TV. They have Internet access at home, school, office, or the local copy shop or cybercafe, using PCs or even their television sets.

Librarians believe that we have a special set of skills to offer. We believe that we can be entrusted to make wise investments to build collections that will serve the needs of our communities. We believe that we can help guide people through a variety of available resources, and help them find the ones that are just right for them. We believe that we can find answers for people with questions, and provide guidance and training to those who want to learn how to find their own.

Society is at as much of a crossroads at the end of the 20th century as it was at the end of the 19th century. Now it's information, rather than education, that's seen as the key to success, and the difference in terminology itself is significant. Education implies knowledge presented within an orderly framework, and information implies that any individual can take information as a raw material and learn whatever he or she needs to know. In an age when almost anyone can have access to the World Wide Web from home, school, office, or even the mall, does anyone need to travel to such a traditional center of learning as the library?

Right now, the answer seems to be "yes," since libraries of all types are busier than ever. People are seeking access to both traditional and electronic forms of information. Reference librarians are helping people use both, and helping people choose information sources based on content, rather than format, and we see people who need coaxing in each direction—from print to electronic and from electronic to print.

As World Wide Web access becomes as commonplace as telephone service, as electronic content and new forms of publishing develop, will we still need libraries and librarians? Only time will answer that question, but certain things are clear. Reference librarians collect, organize, and evaluate information resources, use those resources to find answers for people, and instruct people in using those resources. In an age of greatly increased access to information, and rapid change, those skills are more necessary now than ever. In order to have our skill be recognized, we need to examine every aspect of reference service as it is now delivered: staffing, collections, physical layout, and policies, and work toward a constantly evolving model of reference that will serve the needs of all of our users.

# Chapter 2

# The Changing Role of the Reference Librarian

The essence of reference work is personal service. No matter how well-selected and well-organized our collections are, a library is simply too complex to function well on a self-service basis, and there will be times when our users want personal service. They want help: knowledgeable, skillful, professional, personal help.

The information-seeking behavior of almost all people is the same—if they want to know something, they ask someone. They may ask a friend for personal advice, a trusted expert such as a doctor or lawyer for specialized information, or even a stranger for the time or directions. A reference librarian is someone to ask when you don't know who to ask or when you know you need to look for some specific piece of information and don't know where to begin. A reference librarian is also the person to ask when you thought you would be able to find what you needed, but you can't, or when you have found a lot of information on a subject, but are still missing a few things.

Reference librarians will help when the problem is beyond the resources of your friends, and outside the scope of the doctor, lawyer, accountant, clergyperson, and all the other professionals you can think of. Reference librarians are generally strangers that patrons approach without knowing our names or our qualifications, and they approach us for the same reason that they may approach strangers in other circumstances—they are lost and need directions, and they hope that we know the territory and can point them in the right direction.

Reference librarians also serve people who work independently to find information, but who need a little help from time to time. They may need help learning how to use the information resources we have available, or they may need help when they get stuck at various points in their study. A reference librarian can help the patron get unstuck and continue independent research.

Librarianship as a whole is a helping profession, and nobody in the profession is more involved with providing direct help than the reference librarian. However, it is a helping profession with some distinct differences from such professions as teaching, medicine, and social work. Reference librarians usually help people through many relatively brief encounters, rather than through any ongoing professional relationship.

In addition to working with people, reference librarians also work with human knowledge. And yet, here, too, our relationship with knowledge is different from that of members of other scholarly professions. We are not scientists, scholars, or philosophers, seeking new knowledge; or writers, expressing thoughts and ideas; or teachers, engaged in a long-term process of providing students with intellectual skills and a body of knowledge. We are the ultimate generalists, with many short-term encounters within the world of knowledge, looking up this and that, not necessarily following our own intellectual interests, but rather those of our library users. Even reference librarians working in departmental or special libraries with a special collection are still generalists within a broad subject area.

## CHARACTERISTICS OF REFERENCE LIBRARIANS

Excellent reference librarians share many characteristics, some of which are skills that can be taught or enhanced, but many of which are character traits that the individual brings to the profession.

### Nonjudgmental Desire to Help Others

The reference librarian must have a genuine, unflagging desire to help others achieve their own goals, no matter what those goals may be. We often do not know much about those goals, since we generally only know as much of the context for the question as is necessary to provide an answer, and sometimes that's just as well. Some of our patrons may be using the information that we help them find for purposes that we would personally consider objectionable. Reference librarians need to focus on the patron's immediate need for a fact or help using different kinds of resources, and to provide professional help that is free of our own personal beliefs.

## Curiosity

The excellent reference mind is always wondering about things. It is this quality that enables the librarian to become quickly involved in the needs of library users. No matter what information the patron is seeking, the naturally curious reference mind should be engaged by the question and, at least briefly, the reference librarian should also wonder about the question and be interested in finding the answer. This natural curiosity, coupled with a desire to help others, conveys an attitude of sincere interest to each patron.

## Ability to Shift Focus

This mental agility is a necessary complement to curiosity. While the librarian's mind may be instantly engaged by each new patron's problem, that mind must also be able to drop each query quickly and move on to the next. Often, in fact, the reference librarian is simultaneously juggling several reference problems, and must be able to shift focus to attend to the needs of all, rather than becoming too absorbed in any individual question.

## General Knowledge

There is no substitute for a good general education to help the reference librarian understand and focus questions, especially if that education is supplemented by reading the newspaper, and keeping up on current events, trends, and popular culture. No matter how much knowledge they have, of course, reference librarians will still encounter questions that mean nothing to them without more information, but having a general fund of knowledge to draw upon can be a great help. It can also save time for both the librarian and the patron, which is important in a fast-paced reference department. The more questions you can approach with a little knowledge, the more time you have for the more difficult questions.

### Good Memory

There are two distinct types of memory—long-term and short-term—both of which are important to reference librarians. Long-term memory enables the librarian to have that large general fund of knowledge. Of course, librarians should never answer questions from their own memory, but it's a lot easier to verify a fact that you think you know, or at least have some good clues about, than it is to start every question from scratch.

Short-term memory is what the brain uses to handle information that is needed on a temporary basis. Short-term memory enables the librarian to remember the essential facts, like names and dates, during the course of a reference interview without taking notes, and without forgetting them if another patron asks a question while the librarian is crossing the room to a reference source. Short-term memory also enables the librarian to monitor and offer continuing support to several patrons who are working on different projects, and remember which one was researching the life of Voltaire and which was planning to make a gingerbread version of the House of the Seven Gables.

## Excellent Communication Skills

Reference librarians spend most of their time communicating with a wide variety of library users, in person, on
the phone, by e-mail, and sometimes in other ways. The
encounters may be brief, but they are always purposeful.
The patron wants to know something, and we need to determine just what that is, and to work cooperatively with
the patron to fill that need.

Good one-on-one communication skills are essential to
good service, and as all types of libraries work with an increasingly diverse clientele, these skills become even more
complex and important. However, as information resources are changing so quickly and dramatically, there is
also an increasing need for reference librarians who can
do presentations and training, both for their colleagues and
for patrons. Reference librarians also need to be able to
communicate in writing to prepare press releases and articles promoting library services, and to provide useful content for library guides, pathfinders, and Web pages.

## Patience

Even with excellent communication skills, working with
the public can be difficult, and patience is the quality that
enables reference librarians to maintain their composure
and continue to give good service to patrons who may be
unable to express their needs clearly or who are confused,
unappreciative, rude, or angry. Many people are seeking
information because of situations that are causing them
anxiety: a child custody battle, a medical condition, overdue taxes, or a term paper due tomorrow, and some people

transfer their anxiety into impatience or into hostility toward those who are trying to help them.

Reference librarians need patience to deal not only with difficult patrons but also with the other troublesome circumstances that occasionally fall upon reference departments: paper jams in the printer and flashing toner lights on the photocopy machine, missing volumes of the encyclopedia, and "Unable to Connect" messages on networked PCs. Whatever the circumstances, librarians have to continue to give the best possible service while trying to resolve problems.

### Joy of the Hunt

The joy of the hunt may be the most important quality of all. Reference librarians love the tough questions, and enjoy the challenge of coming up with different approaches to the problem, tracking down clues, and finding an elusive bit of information. They like to solve puzzles, and are persistent and resourceful as they pursue the right answer.

### Creativity

Reference librarians use creative thinking skills to look at a question or problem from many angles and try different approaches to getting to a solution. Reference librarians and their colleagues in other departments also need constantly to look at the library with a critical eye, question why things are done a certain way, and use their creativity to find ways to make changes to improve service. Sometimes an idea that comes in a flash can save hours of time for staff and patrons.

## REFERENCE LIBRARIANS AND OTHER STAFF MEMBERS

Reference librarians have a special role that doesn't often appear on their job descriptions. As they are working with patrons, they are gathering valuable information about the library that can be used to improve services. Many patrons come to reference because they couldn't find what they needed on their own, which is often due to limitations of the collection, problems in cataloging or the design of the online catalog, or lack of signage.

Sometimes, in the course of a conversation with a patron, reference librarians become aware of misunderstandings and problems with circulation, the children's department, interlibrary loan, or other departments of the library. Reference librarians need to achieve a delicate balance, helping the patron without overriding policies of other departments and decisions of other staff members. When it seems appropriate, the reference librarian may want to speak to a supervisor, someone from another department, or a department head to resolve a problem, but this approach always needs to be handled professionally and tactfully. If a situation is likely to come up more than once, a policy for handling it should be worked out between departments and with the library administration, and all should agree to work within those guidelines.

While librarians are working to help patrons, they hear many comments that can be valuable information for planning purposes. Do phone reference patrons mention how many times they have gotten a busy signal or how long they have been on hold? How many patrons mention that they had trouble finding a parking space, or that they love having home access to the library catalog, or that they miss Sunday hours?

Libraries often spend time and money hiring consultants and conducting focus groups and surveys to gather information for planning purposes, while the information gathered from patrons as they actually use the library is lost. This issue is not unique to libraries, of course; it is one we share with other service organizations. Keith E. Ferrazzi, for example, speaking of businesses, writes:

> Focus groups can be very dangerous. They are very often mechanisms to get approval for what you've already made up your mind about. Where you get very good information, frankly, is from your own people on the front lines, from the people who interact with your customers the most. It's much better to concentrate on creating ways to extract that information, codify it, and get it back to where decisions are made (Ferrazzi in Vogl, 1997).

When this kind of information is collected over time, certain patterns emerge that are useful for developing services to meet the true needs of our users. Reference librarians, on the front lines helping our library users, have valuable knowledge that can be used to improve library services.

## CURRENT AWARENESS

A good liberal arts education combined with professional education is a good basic foundation for reference work, but it's only the beginning. Much of reference is not theoretical or academic, it is related to current issues and events, popular culture, sports events, current health concerns, social trends, political issues, technological developments, and so on. State, regional, and local issues are also frequently the context for reference questions, including new or proposed laws or regulations, changes in public transportation, matters under discussion in school districts.

How can reference librarians keep up on all these issues so that they can anticipate patron needs and have a better understanding of the context for questions? To some extent, we rely on the fact that reference staff members read the newspaper and magazines, are active and informed citizens, and are curious and observant about what's going on around them. Reference work itself is a constant education, of course—what you learn helping one patron can become useful knowledge for helping another one.

Reading the newspaper is a great asset to a reference librarian, but it is an activity that few libraries encourage (or even permit) staff members to do on work time. Certainly, having librarians sitting at the reference desk reading the newspaper conveys the wrong image to patrons. However, there are formal and informal ways that libraries can encourage this kind of awareness. For example, having copies of the newspaper and a few general interest magazines available in the staff lounge can provide an opportunity for catching up with the news over coffee. Providing easy access to local, national, and world news sites on the World Wide Web, and making sure that staff members have at least a little free time to spend on networked PCs each day can also help.

Some things, of course, are predictable: elections, the Olympics, the Oscars, the Superbowl, tax time, and holidays, for example. Libraries should use some method or combination of methods to provide ongoing awareness services to all staff members. For example, before the Olympics, all staff members should be reminded when and where the Olympics will be held, whether the library will have any related book displays, book lists, or programs, and what related reference books and other resources are available for patrons. Ideally, of course, many staff members should be involved in preparing for predictable onslaughts of requests.

The methods used for this kind of ongoing awareness service can include staff meetings, printed newsletters or memos, a special bulletin board in the staff lounge or office area, and e-mail. It's helpful if information about reference resources and activities is communicated to all staff members, not just the reference department. The more all staff members know about what's available, the more aware they will be of situations where patrons should be referred to reference.

In addition to communicating information related to these major, predictable events, all staff members should be encouraged to share information they learn about situations likely to lead to reference questions. A news story about a new government program or regulation, which is likely to send people looking for more information and forms, is an example. News stories about local information, including local zoning laws and service club scholarships, are also examples.

Reference librarians need to read the newspaper and listen to radio and television news broadcasts with these questions always in mind: "How is this going to affect members of my community? What further information are they going to need?" When they see stories that are likely

## Keeping Up

Reference librarians need to keep up with news, current events, social issues, technological advances, health issues, hobbies, and everything else that affects the lives of our patrons and sends them off in search of information. In order to do this, every reference librarian should spend several hours a day reading a variety of newspapers and magazines—cover to cover—listening to National Public Radio (NPR) and watching CNN.

Obviously, we need some shortcuts here. Fortunately, there are some great Web sites to help us keep an eye on the world. The following sites, visited regularly, will help reference librarians avoid some of the more embarrassing gaps in current knowledge.

### General News

USA Today
*www.usatoday.com*

*USA Today* is the newspaper that was born to be a Web site. A quick browse around USA Today every day will help you keep abreast of the most important news, lifestyle, health, business, sports, and entertainment stories.

### Current Events and Major Issues

Yahoo's Full Coverage
*headlines.yahoo.com/Full_Coverage/*

As soon as a major news story breaks, Yahoo sets up a Full Coverage page that provides links to individual news stories from major news organizations (including the *New York Times*, *Christian Science Monitor*, CNN and the BBC), audio and video reports from NPR and major television networks, other news sites, related Web sites, and Yahoo categories. These Full Coverage pages provide fast access to important news stories, and offer a variety of ways for readers to follow a story in more depth and from different perspectives.

Perhaps most useful from a reference point of view are the many Full Coverage pages for topics of continuing interest: for example, Affirmative Action, Abortion News, Cancer Research, Social Security Debate.

**Book-Related News**

Amazon.com
*www.amazon.com*

This popular online bookseller's Web site is always worth a visit. Their front page changes frequently, featuring tie-ins to current events, news stories, and deaths of authors and celebrities. The bestseller lists provide a good overview of different subject interests, and the Featured in the Media section includes information on all the books featured on NPR, Oprah, and many general and special interest newspapers and magazines, including *Scientific American*, *National Review*, *Business Week*, and *Wired*.

**Technology**

CNET
*www.cnet.com*

CNET, the computer network, produces a television program and a number of high-quality Web sites, including Snap.com, Builder.com, and Download.com. CNET produces special reports on topics of current interest, such as Linux, PIMs, MP3, and scanners. Their reports are well written and nicely laid out; many of them are aimed as introductions to the nontechnical reader. Regular visits to their main site are a great way to keep up with what's new in technology.

to create a demand for information, they should determine whether the information is readily available in the library, if it can be obtained and made available, or if another agency or organization should be contacted. Then they should inform the rest of the staff. For example: "There was a story in last night's news about sewer tax rebates—information and applications are available from the Office of the Tax Collector at City Hall, [phone number and extension.]"

When teachers notify the library of a class assignment, this information should, of course, be used to evaluate suitable resources, and be shared with the rest of the staff. However, when teachers haven't given us advance notice, reference librarians should gather whatever information about the current assignment they can from the first few students who come in, and share that. If students come in with an assignment sheet or a required reading list, it's helpful to ask the student if you can make a photocopy to keep at the reference desk.

The reference department can have a notebook or folder of current assignments and hot topics, communicate by e-mail, or use a combination of methods. The important thing is that the information is gathered and shared. This kind of awareness service, can greatly improve the confidence and effectiveness of the reference department. This is especially important in a department that includes para-professionals and part-time staff, and can improve the consistency of the service offered at different times of the day and different days of the week.

One outstanding reference awareness service done at the regional level is the web-based newsletter Eureka (*www.gti. net/mocolib1/monthly.html*), edited by Lynne Olver (Figure 2–1). The Morris County Library reference department produces this document as part of its role as Regional Reference Center for the Highlands Library Cooperative. Each issue of Eureka includes articles on several topics important to reference librarians. Some are related to a particular event or time of year, and others are more general. Useful resources are recommended, including a mixture of print, CD-ROM, and Web resources, and referrals to other agencies. The articles in Eureka are always practical, and

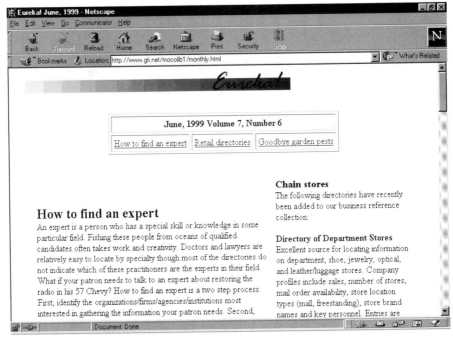

**Figure 2–1. Eureka.**

include not only evaluative information on authoritative sources but also practical tips. For example, the article on income tax information includes information and links for downloading software to handle the Portable Document Format (pdf) and Postscript (ps) files often used for tax forms.

## MANAGING CHANGE

The profession has changed dramatically with the advent of electronic resources, and especially with the Internet, and no one feels these changes more than the reference librarian does. Some are thriving in the new environment, and others are feeling afraid, overwhelmed, stressed-out, and unhappy. This discomfort is especially true for some, though not all, librarians who entered the field more than ten or 15 years ago and who expected to spend their professional lives among books, not computers.

Workstations providing graphical access to the World Wide Web and other resources have brought a host of new problems for reference librarians. The need to protect equipment and enforce acceptable-use policies has caused many libraries to institute sign-on procedures, while the need to provide reasonable access to as many users as possible has caused most libraries to adopt some sort of time limit and scheduling system. Librarians find themselves spending more time administering these systems, and less time assisting users with resources. Librarians also find themselves spending increasing amounts of time maintaining equipment, unjamming printers, restarting frozen workstations, and assisting users with problems that are technical rather than intellectual in nature.

## CHANGED RELATIONSHIPS

In the old days, not so very long ago, most library directors and other administrators had either been reference librarians or had at least had substantial experience at the reference desk, and they were comfortable in the traditional reference environment. Administrators and reference librarians had a shared understanding of reference and could work together on budget, staffing, and supervision issues.

However, in the past ten years, reference work has changed almost beyond recognition. The experience that most administrators had in a more traditional environment is not directly relevant to the problems that their reference librarians are facing. Many administrators who formerly prided themselves on their ability to cover reference themselves if needed, are now uncomfortably aware that they couldn't.

In the past, reference librarians were given a budget for materials, which they spent by selecting materials based on quality, cost, and anticipated need, and while those decisions were sometimes difficult to make, at least the basic issues were clear: for example, which do we need more, this book or that book? In the current, complex and fast-changing environment, however, managing resources involves weighing many different factors. The issues of the actual materials budget may be overshadowed by the issues of managing the workstations and networking necessary to reach and use those information resources.

Since most current library administrators only have reference experience in the pre-Internet environment, they have limited relevant experience to offer in the complicated changes that have come to the reference department. Library administrators must work cooperatively with reference librarians and librarians from other departments to make the best possible decisions to distribute resources (staff, equipment, materials budget) to benefit patrons. This cooperation is only possible when we all acknowledge and understand that in a time of such rapid change, none of us feels as competent, comfortable, and experienced as we are accustomed to feeling.

The fast-changing reference environment has sometimes caused difficult problems within the library staff. Some older staff members, including many supervisors, find themselves uncomfortable in the current library environment. At a time when they expect to be honored and respected for their experience and knowledge, they may find that younger staff members are far more comfortable with computers and especially with the World Wide Web.

The more experienced staff members do have many valuable skills to share, including the ability to understand, interpret, and evaluate information, the ability to communicate effectively with patrons to understand their needs, and the ability to manage staff and budget. However, having younger, newer staff members around who are creating their own Web pages can be unnerving for the older ones who are struggling to learn the new e-mail program and understand the various programs, configurations, options, and glitches that seem to stand between the user and the information itself.

The dichotomy is really not one of age, although it often appears that way. There are certainly older people who are technologically astute and young people who are not. The problem is one of experience and expectations. Librarianship has changed dramatically in the past ten years, and many librarians now find themselves in a profession that they hardly recognize, and perhaps wouldn't have chosen. Reference librarianship used to involve carefully building and maintaining a collection, and working with that collection to help patrons. Now the concept of a collection has less and less meaning, as the move from ownership to access becomes a reality. Reference librarians and our patrons are dealing with a much wider and richer array of information than we ever had before, but one that's constantly changing, and that is accessed through constantly changing programs and protocols.

Reference librarians used to be farmers, tending the fields of information to provide for their users' predictable needs. Now reference librarians are hunters, going out and tracking information as needed, choosing their weapons according to the circumstances.

In reality, of course, reference librarians are, and always have been, both farmers and hunters. In the old days, librarians frequently went off on hunts through the collection and outside of it to track down some elusive piece of promised information, and in the new days, librarians collect, organize, and maintain useful collections of World Wide Web and other electronic resources for our users. But the balance between hunting and farming skills has shifted, leaving many reference librarians with the uncomfortable feeling that they are in the wrong tribe.

## NEW RELATIONSHIPS

Reference librarians have always interacted with each other, with administrators, and, of course, with patrons. Many reference librarians find themselves increasingly involved in some other colleague relationships that can be both rewarding and, at times, frustrating.

### Paraprofessionals

In librarianship, as in a number of other professions, we see a new group of workers gaining attention and recognition. Paraprofessionals in libraries are usually staff members who have a bachelor's degree but do not a master's degree in library science, and they fill a variety of roles performing work that falls between the clerical and professional job roles.

Paraprofessionals may be pursuing a library professional degree or planning to do so, or they may have other long-term goals. Many have advanced degrees or considerable professional experience in another field. Many plan to stay in library work without getting a professional degree. All want the same things as professional librarians: interesting work that we feel is valuable to the community, opportunities to improve our skills, and respect for the work that we do.

Paraprofessionals may have a more difficult time in librarianship than in other professions such as medicine and law, because librarians have had a difficult time establishing professional respect and overcoming image problems. Having paraprofessionals work at the reference desk may seem to discount the complexity and professionalism of reference service. Alicia Barraqué Ellison expresses this point of view in a posting to LIBREF-L: "Librarians have a constant battle to be seen as professionals by the general public. That degree has to count for something."

However, there is another side to the issue of professional status, which is that many tasks in reference may not need the expertise of professional librarians. As the workload and complexity of the department increases, it may be more beneficial to add paraprofessional staff members to allow the professionals more time for other professional activities. Certainly we would all agree that it doesn't take an M.L.S. to put paper in the printer, help patrons with microfilm, or deal with Internet workstation reservations and time limits.

The unresolved issue is whether paraprofessionals should

answer questions for patrons, and whether on-the-job training in the techniques of the reference interview can be an adequate substitute for a professional degree. Many libraries have found that paraprofessionals can do an adequate job, if they are properly trained and supervised, and if there is a clear path for referring the patron to a reference librarian for more help.

Marge Fauver writes that when she was a paraprofessional, she was trained that the proper response for every question (except "where's the water fountain" types) was "I can get you started. There is no librarian available to help you now, but a librarian can lead you to many other resources I am unfamiliar with. Be sure to come back at ____ if you don't find all the information you wanted." Many libraries that have paraprofessionals covering reference alone on nights and weekends encourage them to take the names and contact information of patrons who may need additional assistance.

The ideal situation is the one implied by word paraprofessional. *Para* means "by the side of," and ideally professionals and paraprofessionals should be working together. The paraprofessionals can provide immediate assistance to patrons, referring them to librarians as needed, and can provide ongoing support and assistance to patrons in the stacks or at the workstations.

Professionals should, of course, treat paraprofessionals with respect. Paraprofessionals can go beyond on-the-job training by reading *Library Mosaics* and becoming involved with the library support-staff organizations that are developing and by attending the conferences of the state library associations, many of which offer programs aimed at support staff. The Internet has also become an impor-

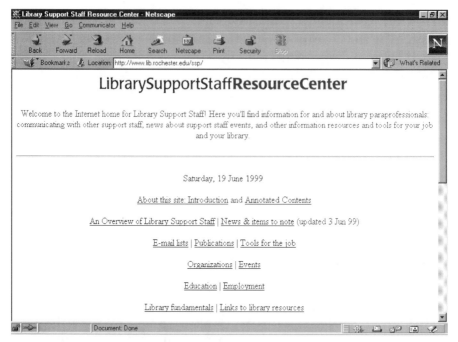

Figure 2–2. The Library Support Staff Resource Center.

tant means of communication and training, through e-mail groups such as LIBSUP-L, the electronic newsletter Associates, and the Library Support Staff Resource Center (*www.rodent.lib.rochester.edu/ssp/*) (Figure 2–2).

### Librarians versus Techies

In all sizes and types of libraries, as reference moves more and more from books to electronic resources, reference librarians are finding themselves working with, and dependent on, a different group of people: the "techies." These technically oriented people may be systems librarians, members of the college computing services department, central site staff of the library system, library support staff hired because of technical expertise, or the staff of various vendors. Whoever they are and whoever they represent, one thing is certain, we are dependent on them for the smooth functioning of our departments, and they don't think the way that we do.

Librarians share a common professional education, and a core of common professional values. We are service oriented, make professional decisions by consensus, and have a tendency toward perfectionism. This perfectionism is one of the underlying factors in our reluctance to use paraprofessionals on the reference desk. What if they are not quite good enough? What if they miss something? We are careful, slow, and deliberate in our approach to many problems. Before we institute a new policy or service, we gather information, evaluate it, and present possible solutions to groups of our colleagues for discussion and revision.

Computing people have a totally different profile. They tend to come from many different educational backgrounds, rather than share a common degree. They are often individualistic and competitive rather than group-oriented and cooperative. They are problem solvers, and are always tinkering and looking for a better way to do things. They thrive on constant change, and are always looking ahead to the next release. They tend to be oriented to the technology rather than to the end user, and to use technical language rather than analogies. When they see a problem, they try to come up with a way to fix it, and will implement their solutions as quickly as possible, often without much testing. They expect users to find and report problems, which they will solve. "Get it out quickly and fix it up as you go along," might be the techie motto—

a sharp contrast to the slower, more deliberate, librarian's approach.

The differences between the two groups is a potential cause of conflict: As Sharon M. West and Steven L. Smith reported on the merger of college library and computing centers:

> Every librarian who has ever worked with a comput-ing person can tell you how they promise and don't deliver, how it never works completely right, and how they never show up when they say they will. Every computing person can tell you how demanding librar-ians are, wanting to know every last little detail and how they insist on every "t" being crossed and every "i" being dotted (West and Smith, 1995).

Real people and real situations are more complex than these generalities suggest, and the differences between "li-brary people" and "computer people" are lessening as technology becomes more mainstream. Nevertheless, many librarians find themselves working in cooperation with technical colleagues who have a different background and perspective on things. Librarians need computer people to design, install, and support the systems we need to fill the rising expectations of our library users. Computer people need librarians to work directly with the end users, to ob-serve how our patrons use systems, think of ways that sys-tems could be improved, and be active in expressing our ideas.

## FOUR STRATEGIES FOR SUCCESS

Change can be stressful, but it can also be exhilarating, freeing, and exciting, as new possibilities emerge and as things that were once impossible become commonplace. Every library needs the skills and experience of many people working together cooperatively and imaginatively to serve our library users.

1. Keep the focus on service.
   Approach every problem from the point of view of the library's users and community, not theoretical considerations, library tradition, or the interests of staff members.

2. Find ways to use the special strengths of individual staff members.
   Sometimes older, more experienced staff who feel less comfortable with the technology make excellent trainers. Their own experience learning to use computers, rather than growing up with them, can make them understand how to break complex things down into simple steps, and their own struggles, plus years of experience working with patrons in other situations, can give them the patience and communication skills necessary for training. Those who were skilled working with the collection itself can be good at selecting and evaluating and organizing World Wide Web resources for pathfinders and Web pages; they can also teach younger staff the evaluative skills necessary in the online environment.

3. Face the facts.

In the past decade, most library jobs have changed dramatically, and there may be staff members—professional, paraprofessional, and support staff—who are so uncomfortable with technology and constant change that they need to consider other options.

4. Acknowledge and respect the different skills people bring to the library.

Respect and communication are essential if we are to work together effectively. Work at understanding how others approach problems, and at helping others understand your own approach. In meetings and discussions, make sure that everyone has a common understanding of a particular problem before people leap to alternative solutions. Encourage everyone to use basic communication skills, including paraphrasing, to make sure that people understand each other's position.

Reference service is essentially personal service; its quality depends on the knowledge, skills, and personal traits of the person delivering that service. Through all the many changes that have come to our libraries, that has remained constant.

# Chapter 3

# Communication Skills

Reference work is the art of making connections between people and the information they need, and to make those connections we need excellent communication skills. This requirement applies at all levels: working with individual patrons to understand their reference questions, working with other library staff members, preparing written material, and giving presentations to groups.

Communication is always a reciprocal process. One person has a thought that he or she wants to share, and chooses words to express it to another person. The second person hears or reads those words and interprets them. To use a sports analogy, one person throws a thought and the other person catches it. Communication is a shared activity, requiring the active participation of both participants. Mortimer Adler wrote that:

> Catching is as much an activity as throwing and requires as much skill, though it is skill of a different kind. Without the complementary efforts of both players, properly attuned to each other, the play can not be completed (Adler, 1983, p. 87).

There are many inherent barriers to communication. The most basic is the fact that we cannot transmit our thought directly, but must use the medium of language. As a message is coded into words by one person and decoded and interpreted by another, a lot of the original meaning can be lost. Language is an imprecise and subjective medium for conveying thoughts. To communicate successfully requires a much more complex interaction than two people just delivering speeches to each other. Even in casual conversation, we use constant direct and indirect verification to make sure that we understand each other's words.

Direct verification happens when the listener repeats or paraphrases a message to make sure he or she understands it, or asks for clarification. Indirect verification consists of all of the nonverbal cues that indicate understanding or confusion, agreement, or disagreement. These include nodding, smiling, frowning, and gestures. Although such nonverbal cues usually facilitate communication, they can also be subject to misinterpretation. Does a raised eyebrow mean interest or skepticism? Does that intent stare indicate disapproval or just concentration? Nonverbal signals are unique and individual, and they also tend to vary among different cultural groups.

Although communication consists of a complex dance of speaking and listening, in our culture much more attention is given to speaking than to listening. Mortimer Adler writes:

> How extraordinary is the fact that no effort is made anywhere in the whole educational process to help individuals learn how to listen well—at least well enough to close the circuit and make speech effective as a means of communication (Adler, 1983, p.5).

Reference encounters present some special communication challenges. Our patrons are coming to us for help, so our communications with them are not conversations, but transactions. They have questions, and we have the responsibility to help them find answers. These are goal-oriented, professional encounters.

Most similar encounters take place within situations where there is an established relationship. For example, a teacher and student may have many conversations that are similar to a reference encounter, but they take place within a larger professional relationship. The same is true of a lawyer and client, or doctor and patient. The two parties are engaged in a contractual relationship. They know each other by name, records are kept, payment is exchanged for services, and the professional is accountable for his or her work.

Information brokers work with their clients in the same type of situation. Special librarians and college and school librarians (especially when they are working with faculty) work in a similar manner. They are not independent contractors, but are serving a known and identifiable clientele, generally in the context of a continuing professional relationship. However, most public library reference work, and much college and school reference work with students, is still "performed on the fly," as a series of brief and often anonymous encounters.

A related communication problem for reference work in a public or general academic library is the lack of context. If I walk into a pet store and say that I am interested in fish, it's obvious by the setting that I am interested in raising fish. In a library, there is no such obvious context, and the question about fish may be about keeping fish, catching fish, studying fish, cooking fish, or even the musical group "Phish."

The lack of a relationship and context also means that both librarians and patrons are guessing at each other's background and knowledge. A customer asking a question about fish in a pet store, for example, can presume that anyone working there has a basic familiarity with the subject, and that he can use the name of a common fish species without clarification. At the general reference desk, where questions may be about any aspect of any subject in the world, we often need a lot of context information from the patron.

Determining the context, of course, is part of the role of the reference interview. But one aspect that we sometimes forget is that our patrons may have trouble approaching us with questions because they don't know how to word their initial request in a setting so devoid of context. Do they assume that we know that Schopenhauer was a philosopher and Poulenc was a composer and Phish is a musical group? There are subtle underlying etiquette issues here. For example, suppose the patron needs help finding information on Poulenc. If the patron just states the question without qualification, there is an assumed risk of embarrassing the staff member who does not recognize the name. If the patron qualifies the name Poulenc by saying "a French composer," there's an assumed risk of offending the staff member who is familiar with the name.

The awkwardness that patrons sometimes feel in framing their initial question is seldom discussed in the professional literature or recognized by librarians, but most reference librarians are immune to this sort of thing. We are not likely to be offended if the patron gives us too much information, or embarrassed if the patron gives us too little. You can't do reference for any length of time without realizing how little you know, and none of us expects to be equally adept at music, art, literature, poetry, sports, politics, and history. A sort of cocktail party conversational etiquette, which requires one to strike a balance between being pretentious and being patronizing, is definitely useful for many of our library users trying to put their question into words.

## WHAT'S THE QUESTION? THE REFERENCE INTERVIEW

The reference interview is the process by which the librarian and the patron arrive at an understanding of what the patron is seeking. It's important to see the patron's initial question as the opening of the dialogue, not the end of it. The patron's real question is the unspoken one: "Am I in the right place? Can you help me? Are you listening to me?"

The literature on the reference interview is filled with examples where patrons are asking misleading and general questions, filled with mistaken assumptions, and the reference librarian is skillfully able to discover the real question. A typical example is the patron who starts by asking where the books on Europe are, but really wants to know when Pompeii was destroyed. Examples are also given of patrons asking for specific reference works, often the wrong ones (like the *Physicians' Desk Reference*, which lists medications, when the real question is about a medical test).

Both situations occur frequently in libraries. Patrons see the reference desk as a place to ask questions, and so they make their best attempt to express their need in the form of a question. Some take a general approach and ask very broad questions, usually asking where books on a general subject are, and others take a specific approach and ask for a particular reference work, which might or might not be of any actual value to them. In either case, the skilled reference librarian should take the time to talk to the patron and try to discern the real information need lurking behind the initial question.

### The Best Approach

The best approach is to ask some questions that will get the patron to share more information. It's usually best to use open questions—ones that require the patron to frame a response in his or her own words—to get to the real question. Closed questions—ones that can be answered with a yes or no or by choosing from a few possible responses— can be too limiting, since they may contain false assumptions about the patron's need. For example, if the librarian asks whether the patron needs information on Beethoven's life or his music, the patron may not volunteer the real need, which is pictures of Beethoven to use in designing a poster.

Sometimes the best question is very open indeed: "Can you tell me more about what you need?" Once patrons have engaged you with the initial question and see that they have your undivided attention, they are often able to explain their situation without much interviewing at all. "Tell me more" is often all that you need to say, as long as the patron can see from your body language that you are listening and are willing to help.

The most important step of the reference interview is to make sure that you and the patron have a common understanding of what the question is before you attempt to locate an answer. Paraphrasing, or repeating the question in your own words, allows the patron to agree that you understand his or her need and to make clarifications or give you additional information if necessary.

### Understanding the Goal of the Question

In real-life reference situations, however, the reference interview may not run as smoothly as it does in role-playing exercises in graduate school. Sometimes the problem is that while we are trying to get to the real information need hiding behind the initial question, there isn't one. Sometimes people really do just want to know where the travel books are and are planning to just browse around looking for inspiration—they do not have a specific question. And some people who ask for a specific reference book have a good reason for doing so. In such cases as these, attempts by a reference librarian to find the "real" question and give better service can often be seen by the patron as puzzling or even intrusive.

Another problem is that many people would prefer not to discuss their information need with a stranger, and would rather frame their requests in general, impersonal terms. Sometimes this is because they are unwilling to share sensitive, personal information about such things as health or legal issues, especially in the middle of a busy public building. Other people just prefer not to discuss their lives with strangers at all, even though their interest in paper airplanes or their upcoming trip to China may not seem like confidential matters to most people.

The trickiest part of the reference interview is the "why" question. It's often helpful to know what the patron intends to do with the information, as a way of understanding the question itself. For example, a patron looking for information about Costa Rica may be writing a paper on political issues in Central America, preparing a speech on saving the rainforest, or planning a vacation. Someone looking for information on a company might be looking for a job or might be making an investment. In each case, understanding the goal of the inquiry is useful because it gives information on the nature of the question.

To clarify the question, reference librarians can ask how the patron intends to use the information, but this must be done carefully—giving the patron the opportunity to maintain privacy—perhaps by focusing on the information needed rather than the patron's actual plans. We should also be careful not to convey the impression that one must always have a specific purpose in mind when seeking our services. Not everybody is writing a paper or planning a project—some people are seeking knowledge for its own sake.

### Starting the Search

Once the patron and librarian agree on what the question is, the search for the answer begins. This process may be a simple matter of looking up a fact in the almanac, but often the reference interview continues into the search process, as sources are explored and the patron refines the question further. Sometimes the best approach when the reference interview seems to stall is to begin the hunt, letting the patron tell you whether you are "getting warmer or getting colder."

Depending on the nature of the inquiry, many people need help getting started and then would prefer to be left alone to go through some material for a time. It's important to check back in a short time to see how they are doing and to offer further assistance if necessary. It's also important for the librarian to offer follow-up assistance, since some people won't come back looking for more help, feeling like they have already had their turn, or not wanting to offend the librarian if the sources offered haven't turned out to be what was needed.

Whether you have found a specific answer for the patron or started the patron off to work on his or her own, the final stage of the reference interview may be the most important—asking if the patron found the information he or she was seeking. The standard format is to ask "Does that completely answer your question?" More important than the specific wording, however, is the tone of voice and body language of the librarian, since the wrong attitude can make this question sound like "Are you finished yet?"

## SERVING MULTILINGUAL PATRONS

Communication can be complex and difficult enough when both parties speak the same language. Language differences can make communication, and therefore good library service, very difficult. Language-related issues are becoming

---

**Three Tips for Good Communication**

The successful reference interview requires some technical skill, such as the use of open questions, the use of paraphrasing to confirm that you understand the question, and the use of a specific, follow-up question, such as "Does that completely answer your question?" to achieve closure.

However, just as important as these technical questions are three basic skills which will improve your ability to communicate successfully with anyone.

1. Deal with the Right Person
   People sometimes come in twos and threes, even when the question really belongs to one of them. Try to identify the person with the question, and deal directly with him or her. This is important even if someone else opens the encounter with a statement like, "My friend here wants to know.." or "My son is doing a report..." Direct the reference interview to the person with the question, not their companion. Young people, old people, and people with any sort of handicap resent the implication that they can't handle their own business—and only the person with the question can work with you to find the right answer.

---

a significant problem for more libraries in our increasingly diverse communities.

Census figures show that the number of United States residents who speak a language other than English at home is increasing. Between 1980 and 1990 the number who speak Spanish grew by 56 percent and the number of Chinese speakers increased 109 percent.

Not only are more of our patrons speaking a language other than English at home; there are now more languages. According to the 1990 census, over 300 languages, from Amharic to Zulu, are the first language spoken at home.

2. Look Them in the Eye, Almost
   Maintaining eye contact is a sign that you are giving someone your full attention, which is essential to the reference interview. In fact, if people feel that they have your undivided attention, they'll often practically interview themselves! Good eye contact also helps you pick up nonverbal cues that help you see whether or not you're on the right track in interpreting their question. Good eye contact, however, means looking at someone's face, with the eyes moving slightly to survey the face and with a focal point between or just above the eyes. Most people are uncomfortable when someone looks directly into their eyes for more than a second or two, and may interpret the look as threatening, intimidating, or suggestive.

3. Follow Their Lead
   You should always maintain a professional demeanor, but that doesn't mean that you have to treat all people the same way. Try to match your style to theirs. Are they formal or informal? Do they seem inclined to chat about their question, or do they have a "just the facts, M'am" minimalist approach? Do they speak in a natural, conversational tone, or with voices lowered to a whisper? The more closely you can attune yourself to the communication style of your patron, the more effective you can be.

The number of languages spoken in the community is more of an issue than the number of people for whom English is a second language. It's a lot easier to provide service to a community where 50 percent of the people are Spanish-speaking than it is for a community where each of ten languages is spoken by 5 percent of the people. It's easier to provide material, signs, and staff in one other language than in ten. And some languages are easier for libraries to deal with than others. For example, many libraries have successfully provided collections and services in Spanish for many years. It's relatively easy to find staff members who speak Spanish, since there are many educated bilingual adults in most of our communities, as well as adults who studied Spanish in high school and college. There are far fewer potential bilingual staff members who speak fluent Latvian, Hmong, or Urdu.

Spanish, Italian, Portuguese, and other European languages are also fairly easy for libraries to deal with because they use the Roman alphabet. Almost all library services, from the catalog to the keyboards used to access electronic resources, are based on that alphabet. Providing services in non-Roman languages, on the other hand, can be extremely complicated and expensive. Romanization schemes used in the online catalog and elsewhere are a compromise that often confuses those patrons who have skill in another language and may be learning English but have no understanding of the transliteration tables.

Libraries are not the only institutions dealing with these difficulties, of course. Schools in some ways have a more acute problem than libraries. Coming to the library is a voluntary act; most people who believe that they cannot get service in their own language will simply avoid the library. School attendance, however, is compulsory whether or not the school is equipped to communicate with a child in the language spoken at home. California's Santa Clara County public schools, for example, serve students who speak over 50 different languages, and prints report cards and notices in four of them.

Some banks make a concerted effort to reach out to minority communities. First Bank in the Minneapolis–St. Paul area employs tellers who speak a variety of languages including Korean, Vietnamese, Cambodian, Thai, Spanish, and Russian. Norwest Bank, in the same area, also has multilingual ATM machines in the Hispanic and Hmong communities, and offers 24–hour multilingual telephone banking through an AT&T language line.

Some libraries have made outstanding efforts to provide services to all of the people in the community. New York City's Queens Borough Public Library is a leader in this area. Queens is the most ethnically diverse of New York's five boroughs, with almost half of the population speaking a language other than English at home. The library's New American Program includes substantial collections in Spanish, Chinese, Korean, and South Asian languages as well as popular books in many other languages.

Queens also offers the largest library-managed English as a Second Language program in the country, annually serving nearly 3,000 students from over 80 countries and speaking over 50 languages. In addition, the library offers lectures and workshops in many different languages, aimed at providing new immigrants with information on such topics as citizenship and job training to help them adjust and succeed in their new homes. There are also programs celebrating the arts and culture of different areas of the homelands of residents of Queens.

### Multilingual Electronic Resources

The use of computers, especially Internet-connected computers, has quite literally brought a new world of resources to our patrons. Not only can our patrons find information in their own languages, they can find sources in their own homelands.

For example, many libraries with a sizeable Spanish-speaking population subscribe to one or two Spanish-lan-

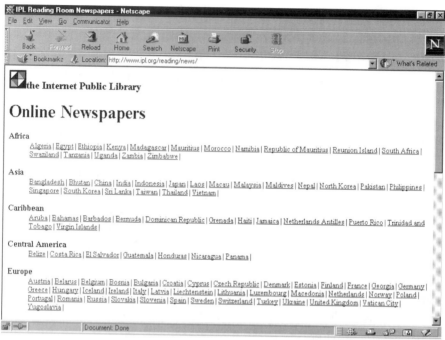

Figure 3–1. The Internet Public Library's Directory of Online News-papers.

guage newspapers, but now all libraries with Internet access can provide access to Spanish-language news sites that range from major, general sites, like CNN En Español (*cnnenespanol.com/*) to the Web sites of newspapers and television and radio stations many different Spanish-speaking countries. These sites may be simple, offering just the day's headlines, or as sophisticated as Puerto Rico's El Nueva Dia Interactivo (*www.endi.com/*).

Access to these local news resources is a great benefit to our patrons. American news sources generally cover only the most dramatic of news stories from other countries, and those with a minimum of detail. Homeland news,

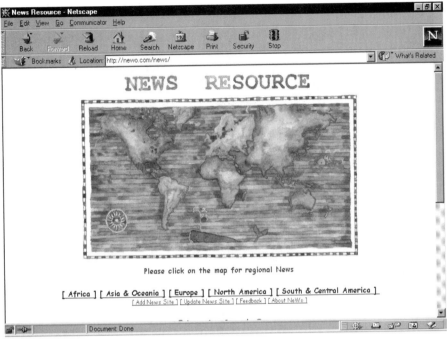

**Figure 3–2. News Resource: NeWo's Directory of Worldwide News Services.**

accessed directly, can help our patrons keep in touch with the countries and people that they left behind. The Internet Public Library (Figure 3–1) maintains a well-organized collection of links to online newspapers around the world (*www.ipl.org/reading/news/*) and NeWo's News Resource page (*newo.com/news/*) provides access to a wider assortment of news resources from around the world, including the online sites of newspapers, television and radio stations (Figure 3–2).

Beyond news, of course, there are all kinds of World Wide Web sites and services in many different languages that can serve the intellectual, practical, and recreational needs of our patrons. In many ways, by connecting to the Internet, libraries of all types and sizes have instantly acquired access to a vast collection of resources in hundreds of languages, making it much easier than ever for us to serve our diverse patrons.

And yet, providing access to multilingual resources presents many new difficulties. Patrons using Internet workstations often get stuck and need help, with problems that may be technical or resource-related or some combination of the two, which can be trying when the patron and the librarian do not speak the same language, or when the librarian can't understand what's written on the screen.

Dealing with Russian, Chinese, Japanese, Korean, and other languages that don't use the Roman alphabet presents a host of problems. The software needed for the PC to interpret other character sets is free or inexpensive, but setting up and maintaining the configurations for several different languages can be complicated, time-consuming, and frustrating for both the library staff and the patron. Many languages have two or three different encoding systems, and the software must be properly configured and invoked to handle various pages. The Queens WorldLinq project includes workstations with Asian-language software at the Central Library and many branches, and they have written clear instructions for creating and viewing Chinese, Japanese, and Korean pages—but with the variations of page encoding techniques, there's no way to make this process simple.

Some sites use an alternative method of handling text—instead of language-encoding systems, they use various kinds of image technology, creating something that is not text, but a picture of text. There are problems with this

## Language Help for the World Wide Web

There's a reason that they call it the *World Wide* Web, and your library users will find information from all over the world, in many different languages. Eventually, we hope, the new standard called UNICODE will make it possible for all World Wide Web browsers, e-mail clients, and other programs to move seamlessly from one language to another. In the meantime, we have an extended character set to deal with characters like the tilde and umlaut, and a variety of separate encoding schemes used for non-Roman languages. Some languages have more than one encoding scheme—Chinese pages from the mainland usually use GB (or Traditional) encoding, while those from Taiwan and Hong Kong usually use Big 5 (or Simplified) encoding.

Many people configure their own PCs to access an encoding scheme beyond Western, which accommodates English and other Roman-alphabet languages. Likewise, public workstations in libraries may need to access many different languages to accommodate the needs of our polyglot patrons.

The best source of information on setting up different language systems is the one most overlooked: the help system of the browser itself. In Netscape Communicator 4.5, for example, choose the option called International Users in the Help menu.

### Chinese/Japanese/Korean

Chinese, Japanese, and Korean all require much larger character sets than alphabet-based languages like Greek or Russian, and it's worth the money to invest in CJK language suite software. Users need to launch the program and select a language and encoding scheme to view Web pages. NJ Star and Asian Suite are two of the most popular CJK programs. Both programs can be downloaded for a free trial from the vendor sites below:

NJ Win: *www.njstar.com*
Asian Suite: *www.unionway.com/*

*Continued on following page*

---

**Russian**

Russian is easier to set up than Chinese, Japanese, and Korean, and you'll find simple, step-by-step directions on the Russify Everything page (*www.siber.com/sib/russify/*) at SovInformBureau. If you want to read even more about this topic, try Paul Gorodyansky's Useful Cyrillic (Russian) Stuff (*ourworld. compuserve. com/homepages/Paul_Gorodyansky/*), which includes clear instructions for using different Russian keyboard layouts, using Russian in Office 97, and more. If you want to read *less* about this, you may want to consider a product like the Cyrillic Starter Kit from Fingertip Software (*www.fingertipsoft.com/cyrstart/*).

**Other Languages**

There are two great starting points for information on non-English languages. The Human Languages Page (*www.june29.com/HLP/*), by Tyler Chambers, is a large, annotated and well-organized collection of links for many languages. The Yamada Language Guides (*babel.uoregon.edu/yamada/guides.html*), maintained by the Yamada Language Center of the University of Oregon, includes a large font archive and extensive information on language configuration issues.

---

approach: it can be slow, the text is not searchable, and it requires intermediary processing to convert text to images. But in some circumstances it can be an effective way of bypassing the problems of language encoding.

For example, the Boston Russian Bulletin (*www. russianmass.com*) makes its current issue available using Adobe's Portable Document Format, (pdf) which can be displayed and printed using the free Acrobat Reader, commonly used for tax forms and other documents that must retain their original format. They plan to provide alternative means of access, but this method allows them to scan and convert the Bulletin and make it instantly and easily available on the World Wide Web without any encoding issues.

The Shodouka Launchpad (*www.shodouka.com*) uses a different approach, serving as an intermediary between the user at a PC without Japanese-language software installed and the Japanese language site. A user enters the URL for any Japanese language site into a box on the main page of this site, or selects Yahoo! Japan or one of the other popular Japanese pages listed there. Shodouka retrieves the Japanese page, runs it through its own special software, which interprets the Japanese text and then converts it to image files in GIF (Graphics Interchange Format) format; Shodouka then sends the page, with images replacing the text, back to the user's browser, which displays it like any other page with images.

Shodouka provides this free service on a page supported by advertising as a way of familiarizing users with its commercial software product, which can be licensed to run on a local computer system to convert Japanese-language pages instantly, without the inevitable delay of going through an intermediary site.

All of these approaches to handling different languages can greatly benefit our users, but they also add technological and support burdens for library staff. Even more difficult, perhaps, for librarians is the sense that all of these resources from around the world are so near, and yet so far. We know they are there, if only we can figure out how to access them. With print resources, in contrast, if someone asked us if we could provide access to information in Japanese, we knew the answer to that question, and whether the answer was "yes," "no," or "no, but we can borrow some from another library."

Now we may not even know the answer to the question—we may not be sure if our browsers have been configured to handle Japanese text, and if they have, how to use this feature properly. Or we may tell a patron, apologetically, that "no, we do not have Japanese-language software on our browsers, and therefore one can't view Japanese pages on our workstations," confident that we have given a true, if regrettable answer. But the next day, we may see another patron or staff member successfully reading Japanese by using the Shodouka Launchpad. The difficulty of keeping up with what is possible—and therefore, what we can offer patrons—is a great source of stress for reference librarians.

### Translation Aids

There are many different types of translation aids available, which can be helpful at the reference desk. The most basic, least expensive, aids are small, handheld electronic devices that contain dictionaries and basic translation capabilities for one or more languages. A more effective solution is the use of a professional translation service. AT&T's Language Line Services (*www.att.com/languageline/*) provides professional translation over the phone in 140 different languages. This high-level service is frequently used by businesses, hospitals, and police departments.

AltaVista's Translation Assistant (*babelfish.altavista.digital.com*) is an interesting development (Figure 3–3). You can connect to this free site and input either a short piece of text, either from the keyboard or by cutting and pasting from another page or file, and choose to have the passage translated to or from English and French, German,

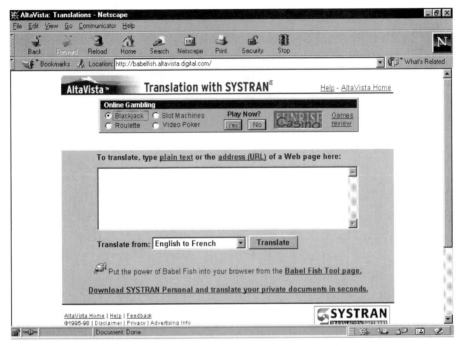

**Figure 3–3. Babel Fish: AltaVista's Translation Assistant.**

Italian, Spanish, and Portuguese. You can also input a URL, and Translation Assistant will retrieve the page and translate it. Think of the possibilities: for librarians and patrons to search and retrieve Web pages and have them translated on the fly, or even to communicate by typing messages into Translation Assistant and having them translated.

It should be noted that translation is an art not easily performed by software, and that conversion programs yield a rough translation at best. Complex sentence structure, words with multiple meanings, and idioms are especially difficult for the software to handle. Translation software is improving, however, and a service like this can be an aid to communication in some circumstances. It may, for example, be good enough to enable the patron to locate a document in a language he doesn't know, confirm that it contains the needed information, and print it out to take elsewhere for a better translation.

### Other Language Issues

Serving the needs of multilingual patrons may raise some political issues for the library, even among members of the library staff. Many people believe that it is essential for immigrants to learn English as quickly as possible, and that any support for the use of the original language impedes the learning process and is an unreasonable burden on tax-payers. Several states and many cities have enacted laws or amendments declaring English their official tongue, which may make it difficult for public libraries and librar-ies in public schools to justify signs, brochures, and Web pages in languages other than English.

These political issues can be difficult for reference librar-ians, who may find themselves in the middle. For those who work directly with patrons, the issue of support for multiple languages is not political, but practical.

## COMMUNICATION CHALLENGES

Libraries are serving an increasingly diverse clientele in ev-ery sense. We are working with many people who have handicaps, problems, or other situations that present com-munication challenges.

Some patrons have limited English skills or they may

have accents that make it difficult for us to understand them. (In fact, native English speakers can be difficult for another to understand if they are from a different area.) It may be difficult for us to assess how well a person understands English, since speaking ability and oral comprehension are separate skills. It's difficult to strike a balance between overestimating someone's language skills (and rattling on rapidly, totally losing the patron) or underestimating the comprehension level (addressing the patron with great, deliberate slowness and care). Worst of all is the tendency that some people have to speak not only slowly, but loudly, and with exaggerated simplicity: "YOU WANT BOOK? YOU WANT BOOK FOR COOKING?"

Encounters with patrons with limited English or difficult accents are stressful situations for reference librarians, but they are more stressful for the patrons themselves. There is no magic technique for these situations, but common sense, patience, and resourcefulness all help. Encourage the patron to repeat his or her request, slowly, while you listen carefully and repeat what you think you are hearing. Moving with the patron to a quieter area can help, since the sounds of others talking can be distracting to both of you.

The situation can be frustrating for both the patron and the librarian, but it's important to treat the situation in a matter-of-fact manner as just another problem to be solved. It may be helpful to have the patron write down the question, or at least the few key words that seem to be a problem. If the patron is having trouble coming up with a certain word in English, you may want to offer a bilingual dictionary of the patron's own language. In some cases, another staff member can be asked to assist.

In "Dealing with International Students in a Multicultural Era," Kwasi Sarkodie-Mensah (1992) encourages librarians to take a more proactive approach to serving students from other countries. Librarians can increase their ability to understand patrons from different backgrounds by learning the characteristic language problems of different groups. Spanish-speaking people tend to add an "e" sound before the initial letter *s*, Arabic people have the tendency to substitute *p* for *b* and vice versa, and Japanese students have a similar tendency with *r* and *l* sounds. Understanding such basic language pattern differences can make it much easier to interpret a patron's words without resorting to paper and pen.

Sarkodie-Mensah also suggests that there would be fewer "tense encounters of the foreign kind" in reference if more librarians were to take just one class in a foreign language or culture.

> People would come to realize how tiresome speaking in another language is; how much effort is required. . . . Librarians would grow more patient with, less frustrated at, and more receptive to patrons who may require more time at the desk, in the classroom, or any setting where requests for information are made, (Sarkodie-Mensah, 1992).

The same common-sense techniques are also important in working with patrons who stutter, have a speech impediment, have had a laryngectomy, or are difficult to understand for any reason. Patience and a matter-of-fact attitude are important. The librarian may feel embarrassed and frustrated by his or her inability to catch what the patron is trying to say, but displaying this embarrassment only causes the patron additional stress and impedes the process of reaching an understanding.

## Mainstreaming

The Americans with Disabilities Act (ADA) and changes in society have benefited many people with various handicaps of sight, hearing, and mobility. Handicapped people used to be marginalized in various ways. Deaf and blind students generally attended special schools, where specialists met their library needs; now these students are generally mainstreamed in both schools and libraries. Many handicapped adults were unemployed or underemployed, but increasingly they are fully employed, active in society, and have the same range of information needs as our other patrons. Architectural barriers used to keep us from seeing many handicapped patrons, but as these barriers are eliminated, we serve an increasingly diverse clientele and thus face some new communication issues.

The move to electronic resources has opened many new opportunities for libraries to serve visually handicapped people. Rather than rely on special secondary formats, like Braille and talking books, libraries can use adaptive technology to allow patrons direct access to the same body of resources as everyone else. Adaptive technology for the visually impaired is complex and rapidly evolving. Instead of being viewed on a screen or printed on paper, adaptive technology allows electronic text to be output as speech, Braille, or in a variety of other formats. The move from the text-based DOS to graphical user interfaces brought new complications and new solutions to the designers and users of adaptable technology. There are also many different adaptive programs and devices for physically handicapped people, allowing even people with very limited mobility to operate a computer. The new possibilities for service are exciting, but require planning, training, publicity, and evaluation for successful implementation.

Many libraries respond to ADA requirements by setting up an adaptive technology center. However, it's important to make sure that all of the materials that a patron might need can be accessed in this center. Some barriers to access are technological, while others are a matter of policy. For example, David W. Wilhemus has described some of his experiences as a visually impaired law student and graduate student of librarianship, in universities with adaptive technology centers. In one case, he was unable to access WESTLAW and LEXIS/NEXIS for class assignments, because these services could only be accessed from terminals in the reference area, not in the adaptive technology center one floor above. In another, the policy of the law library would not permit print material to be borrowed for use in the technology center a block away (Wilhemus, 1996).

In accordance with the requirements and the spirit of the Americans with Disabilities Act, most libraries are making an effort to provide adaptive technology solutions for patrons in our buildings. Libraries should also reach out to users who may be confined to their homes, or who may prefer to access library resources from home where they have a computer specifically configured to their own needs and preferences. Many such patrons have modems and often Internet access, and can benefit from access to the library catalog, periodicals databases, and other library services, including reference service via e-mail.

## FOUR STRATEGIES FOR SUCCESS

Communication is an essential element of good reference service. All staff members should be trained to use good professional communication techniques, and the library should make adequate provision for services to users with special communication issues.

1. Always perform a proper reference interview, and encourage others to do the same.

   The three essential elements of the reference interview are using open questions, paraphrasing to make sure you understand the question, and achieving closure by asking the patron if the question has been completely answered. These techniques can be taught to almost anyone—the hard part is making sure they are used consistently by all staff members who do reference work. Staff members should be reminded if necessary to use all three techniques, and they should be evaluated on their use of these techniques.

2. Have a policy and a plan for serving library users with limited English skills.

   All reference staff members should know what translation services are available to them, and how to access those services. Such services could range from a professional translation service to volunteers in the community who are available on call. Lists of basic messages in different languages spoken in the community should be prepared for use with patrons whose English is limited.

3. Make sure that workstations are equipped for multilingual support and that all staff members are trained
   in how to use this.
   It is not expensive or difficult to set up workstations
   to handle multiple character sets, especially Cyrillic
   (for Russian language support) and CJK (for Chinese,
   Japanese, and Korean), but it does require some preparation, maintenance, and training.

4. Learn more about special communication issues.
   Invite professionals and members of the community
   to help the staff learn more about working with people
   who are hearing-impaired or have other communications problems. Work with others in the community
   to develop adaptive technology programs, and make
   sure that all staff members receive training and support in the use of these systems, and that the public
   is aware of what's available. Review adaptive technology programs at least annually, with input from
   members of the community.

Communication issues can cause embarrassment and
frustration for both the librarian and the library user, thus
preventing us from giving good service. Fortunately, communication skills can be learned, and software and hardware solutions are available to help us with some of the
most difficult problems.

# Chapter 4

# Resources

Reference librarians are only as good as their collections. We never answer questions from our own memory, but always find answers in appropriate sources, verify them if possible in another source, and present the answers and citations to our patrons. We also introduce our library users to our reference collections and assist them in performing their own research. For many decades, the reference collection consisted almost totally of reference books, including many annuals editions of standard works from a few well-respected reference publishers. In the past ten years, however, reference collections have been transformed by the move from print to electronic resources.

## A BRIEF HISTORY OF THE REFERENCE COLLECTION

Until the last decade, reference collections were developed in an orderly, traditional manner. Librarians selected materials to purchase for the use of their patrons. Funds were always limited, so careful choices had to be made. Librarians made selection decisions based on knowledge of the interests of the community, the strengths and weaknesses of the current collection, and the quality of available material. They read reviews, and sometimes previewed the actual material. Books were purchased for both the general library collection and for the reference collection.

As new books were received, librarians examined them, cataloged them, and added them to the collection. Reference librarians would examine new reference books closely, looking at the scope, organization, and indexing of the new works. Most libraries had a formal or informal system of ensuring that all reference staff members would examine new reference books as they arrived.

In addition to books, we dealt with periodicals, which presented some additional problems. We cataloged serial titles, but relied on professional indexing services to provide access to the content of the periodicals. However, most of us only used a few different indexes, and most of us were very comfortable using the *Readers' Guide to Periodical Literature* and some specialized indexes, and showing patrons how to use them. New volumes would arrive, but the format and organization (and even the color) stayed the same.

Many libraries collected other material in vertical files. Collecting and organizing pamphlets, brochures, pictures, maps, and other small sources of information was time-consuming but rewarding. Other formats of information, including sound and videorecordings, entered the library world, but they were primarily browsing, circulating collections. With a few exceptions, like sound recordings of famous speeches or national anthems, these materials were not generally used in reference work, although reference librarians worked with these collections to some extent, in their general role of helping patrons use the catalog and find needed material.

Photocopiers and microforms presented new opportunities and some new problems. Librarians were now responsible for teaching patrons how to operate a piece of equipment, rather than how to understand the intellectual content and organization of a reference book. The photocopy machine proved surprisingly challenging for many patrons, who often had a hard time lining up their document or book pages to fit on the paper. Patrons were also confused by the fact that they had to deal with different models of photocopy machines, so that the buttons were never quite where they expected them to be, and the more features that the machine had, the harder it was for some users to find the Print button.

Microfilm reader/printers were also difficult for many users, and sometimes for staff members who had to deal with things like rolls of microfilm that had been rewound backward on the spool. Although librarians did have to spend time helping patrons use photocopy machines and microform readers, the machines themselves were relatively simple, and the help needed was usually brief, just enough time to get a patron started. There was no continuing interaction between the information and the machine that required further help or explanation.

In addition to equipment instruction, microforms and their reader/printers introduced another element into reference librarianship: equipment dependence. If the microfilm reader was out of service for some reason, the entire collection of microfilm was useless. Since microfilm was almost always a replacement format, rather than a supplement to print copies, this was a serious service issue, and librarians responded in two ways: building redundancy into the system by having more than one machine if possible (and more than one bulb on hand!) and by making sure the machines were maintained and serviced regularly and replaced when they became unreliable.

When CD-ROMs and online database services came along, they were eagerly embraced by most reference librarians. These tools greatly expanded the services that we were able to offer, but they still fit into our traditional pattern. They were resources that we reviewed, evaluated, and selected within the limits of our budget. We learned how to use the ones that we had selected and trained our patrons in their use. Although we had moved from buckram binding to a computer workstation, working with products like InfoTrac used the same general set of skills as working with the *Readers' Guide*: we selected it, mastered its system, added the updates, and taught patrons how to use it effectively.

The PC workstations that were used for CD-ROMs presented us with more equipment issues, both in terms of maintaining equipment and training patrons. With the indexes, technical and intellectual skills were intertwined. We had to help patrons with both the interface and the indexing: What is a keyword and where do I type it in? How do I limit a search by date and why would I want to do that? How can I print this list of citations?

The CD-ROM databases brought some other new issues. Librarians needed to think of ways to compare the cost of the CD-ROM product with the cost of similar print products. Some aspects, such as the number of titles indexed, were easy to compare, but other aspects were more complicated. Only one person could use the CD-ROM at a time, but several could use the print indexes if they were using different volumes. And which was easier to use, the print indexes or the CD-ROM versions? The CD-ROM products had much more sophisticated sorting and searching, but when they were first introduced, many patrons had limited experience with computers and preferred the familiar book format. Also, the CD-ROM products, like microfilm, were dependent on a piece of equipment. What would happen if the equipment failed? What would happen if the company stopped producing the CD-ROMs, or if the CD-ROM format itself went the way of 8–track tapes?

With the advent of the Internet, and especially the World Wide Web, everything changed. With the World Wide Web, you do not select individual resources; you gain access to the Web itself, and you have access to everything that has been made available on the Web. Librarians have lost much of their role as selectors of resources and have gained a complex new role as managers of access to resources.

## REFERENCE BOOKS

Even with the great increase in electronic reference resources, most libraries still maintain a large collection of reference books. What makes something a reference book? The term has a few different, overlapping meanings. One refers to the purpose of the book itself—a reference book is a "look-up book" (one that is designed to be consulted, rather than read). Another meaning relates to its use in the library—in most libraries, reference books are books that do not circulate, but must be used in the library.

There are some good reasons to maintain a collection of books that must remain in the library. A reference collection can be viewed as an inconvenience to patrons, forcing them to stay and work in the library rather than in the privacy and comfort of their own homes. However, without retaining certain materials in the library at all times, we cannot ensure having a core of material that is always available for patrons to use when everything else on their topic has been checked out, and for librarians to use in answering walk-in and telephone reference questions.

Some libraries have policies that prevent reference books from ever being removed from the library. Some allow short-term loans, usually overnight, under special circumstances. Many libraries respond to the needs of patrons to use reference material at home by buying duplicate copies of reference titles for the circulating collection, or by moving older editions into the circulating collection when new editions are received for reference.

Such decisions should be made carefully and considered from the patron's point of view, and with an understanding of how patrons use different types of material. For example, the annual *Writer's Market* is found in the reference collection of most libraries. Its format is certainly that of a reference book, since it is a directory of entries for publishers of books, magazines, and other material, with contact names, addresses, and current editorial needs. However, unlike many directories, most people using this book do not want to check one or two entries; they want to spend time going through many entries, studying the markets. Thus, this is a book that most patrons would prefer to use at home rather than at the library.

Many libraries respond to this need by allowing the older editions to circulate, but in this case, the older edition is not just a little outdated—it is useless. Publishing is a volatile profession, with new publications—prime markets for freelancers—coming into being and editors frequently changing position. *Writer's Market* is more than a listing of publications; it also lists each publication's current needs. Once a need is listed, freelancers rush to fill it. If a children's magazine is looking for brief biographies of women one year, it will usually receive more than it needs, and the following year will list something entirely different. Last year's *Writer's Market* is of no more use to patrons than month-old real estate ads or job postings. Current copies of *Writer's Market* and similar marketplace works are prime candidates for the circulating collection, especially since they are produced primarily for the home rather than library market, and are not particularly expensive.

There's no general rule, however, on how to maintain an adequate reference collection while also serving the needs of patrons who want material they can use at home. Reference librarians need to cooperate with other staff members in collection development, considering each category of material and deciding whether a title should be added to the reference collection, the circulating collection, both collections, or whether this is an instance where moving older editions from reference to the circulating collection makes sense.

Maintaining the reference collection is a complex and

time-consuming task. The collection is likely to be a mix of individual monographs and serials, which may or may not be on standing order. David R. Majka, in his article "Developing an Electronic Tickler File for Reference Collection Management," describes the literature on the subject:

> Various authors employ pejoratives such as time-consuming, dusty, frustrating, endless, discouraging, labor-intensive, tedious, and arduous to describe this process . . . work done only under the duress of full stacks or prior to a visit by the accreditation team. This agonizing process usually is insufficient to keep up with new editions, doesn't focus attention on the books most in need of replacement—many times the oldest volumes in the reference collection—and makes the reference stacks a purgatory for the unfortunate staff who have to perform this work (Majka, 1995).

Majka's tickler file method of reference collection management works on a separate database of records for each reference title. In many ways it's similar to the traditional practice of making notes on the shelflist cards for reference titles, but it includes the important and often neglected feature of recording collection management decisions by date and staff member, so that reports can be generated for titles not reviewed within a specified amount of time.

This is an area of collection management that deserves more attention and innovative solutions. Reference librarians need to work with technical services librarians, systems librarians, and systems vendors to design processes that automate as much of the routine work as possible.

Perhaps whenever a reference title is added to the collection, it should be coded with a removal date, similar to the "sell by" dates on perishable items. If we want to maintain current collections of information for our users, we need to be active in seeking better ways to remove and replace outdated material.

## READY REFERENCE COLLECTIONS

Many libraries maintain a special subset of the reference collection as what is generally known as a ready reference collection. This collection may consist of a few almanacs and a dictionary on top of the reference desk or an entire stack range of materials behind it. As the name suggests, books are generally assigned to this special collection so they will be close at hand for answering patrons' quick questions in person or on the phone. Other books may also find their way into this collection (due to recurring mutilation or loss) to be under the watchful eye of the reference staff. *Grzimek's Animal Life Encyclopedia* and various style manuals are frequently mentioned candidates for this type of protective custody.

Although having certain titles near the reference desk can be helpful to staff, it can be inconvenient to patrons. Ready reference books are either given a special designation in the catalog or some type of placeholder (such as dummy blocks) is used to refer patrons from the regular reference shelves to the desk. Either method tends to confuse patrons. Both patrons and staff are inconvenienced if patrons have to ask at the desk for frequently used items, and patrons are less likely to ask at the reference desk to use an unfamiliar ready reference source than they are to take it off the reference shelf and look at it. Some of the inconvenience to patrons can be relieved by having copies of a book in both the reference and the ready reference collections, but this approach is not always practical with more expensive material.

The natural tendency of such ready reference collections seems to be to grow to fit the amount of available space. Books are often assigned to ready reference and remain there permanently despite changes in staff and circumstances. Such collections should be periodically evaluated to see whether they are productive or counterproductive for both staff and patrons. Such an evaluation can also serve to evaluate which sources staff members are using most frequently, and whether these are the most appropriate. For example, some staff members may be relying on almanacs and similar sources for information that is more current and accurate on the World Wide Web or in a reference database.

Juleigh Muirhead Clark and Karen Cary describe an interesting experiment at the James Branch Cabell Library of Virginia Commonwealth University. The ready reference collection had grown to unwieldy proportions, with the staff spending an inordinate amount of time exchanging identification cards for high-use ready reference books. A plan was needed to evaluate the ready reference collection and to reduce its size. Although the staff considered the idea of having a series of staff meetings to review the collection on an item-by-item basis, it seemed likely that this method would be too time-consuming to be productive, and so a different approach was used. All but a few of the ready reference titles were moved into the general collection, with the wooden dummies moved to the reference desk. Staff members were given the option of reassigning books to the ready reference collection as needed. Only a small percentage of books were brought back to the reference desk.

Although the main goal of the project was to reduce the amount of time the staff devoted to handing reference books across the desk to students, Clark and Cary note an additional benefit from the reduction of the size of the desk collection. With fewer books at hand, the reference staff is less likely to rely on this subset of the reference collection, and more likely to go into the reference collection and use the most appropriate source or sources to answer questions (Clark and Cary, 1995).

## ACCURACY AND BIAS

Librarians actively seek a variety of material for our circulating collections, attempting to represent various points of view. We tend to hold the reference collection to a much different standard from the general collection, however. Since we use it to answer reference questions, we are much more concerned about accuracy, currency and authority.

Certain types of material, such as books that are in a standard reference format but that have a pronounced point-of-view, may raise troublesome issues within the library. For example, *The Encyclopedia of the Palestine Problem*, was the subject of a lively and thought-provoking discussion on LIBREF-L. Anne Berwind of the Woodward Library, Austin Peay State University, raised the issue after the library received the work as a donation from the

Palestine Arab Delegation. Noting the book's apparent
strong pro-Palestine, anti-Zionist bias, she wrote:

> I am not advocating censorship of this work and don't
> want to open the whole Pandora's box of the library
> bill of rights, freedom of information, academic free-
> dom, etc. But, at the same time, I hesitate to simply
> place this title on the DS 119.7 shelf in the reference
> collection because it might give it more credibility and
> legitimacy than a biased work deserves. Can we re-
> ally expect undergraduates to make the judgments nec-
> essary to use this kind of material? Perhaps it would
> be easiest to place it in the circulating collection, or
> would that make matters worse?

Most respondents were from academic libraries, and
most concluded that multiple points of view should be represented in the reference collection, as well as the circulating collection, noting that undergraduates should be able
to determine and evaluate the bias of this and other reference works. Jeff Beck, of the Wabash College Library,
notes that, "It is pretty clear to any reader that this source
is different in its attempt to be persuasive . . . I am much
more concerned with works in which the bias is more in-
vidiously subtle."

Some sources have problems that go beyond bias or
point of view. What responsibility, if any, do libraries have
for handling academic fraud? There have been numerous
well-documented incidents in recent years of reports based
on fraudulent data or other types of academic misconduct.
Most librarians believe that the peer-review process is an
effective safeguard against academic misconduct, and some

academic databases allow searches to be limited to peer-reviewed journals. However, Arnold Relmen, former editor of the *New England Journal of Medicine*, observed that unless a "maladroit cheat" fabricated results that were obviously impossible or contradictory, even rigorous peer review is unlikely to reveal fraud (Relmen, 1983).

Even when fraud is uncovered, libraries generally continue providing access to *the original articles*. This is in concert with the American Library Association's Statement on Labeling. MEDLINE, however, adds the type of publication designation "Retraction of Publication" to citations for articles formally retracted by the author or the editor of the journal.

Beyond academic fraud, of course, accuracy can be suspect for other materials in our collections. These include everything from academic articles based on flawed (as opposed to dishonest) research studies to outdated hotel and restaurant guides. Reference books are occasionally even subject to recall, as in the case of the 19th edition of the American Kennel Club's venerable *The Complete Dog Book*. The book was recalled after protests over breed profiles that listed a number of popular breeds as being not suitable for children.

Ultimately, it is the responsibility of our library users to evaluate the accuracy of the information they find in our libraries, but librarians should certainly work toward providing the best collections for our users, and have an understanding of the issues of accuracy, including fraud, invalid research, bias, and superceded material, and be prepared to provide guidance to patrons in using our collections.

## CREATING OUR OWN REFERENCE RESOURCES

Sometimes librarians know that certain reference resources are needed but are not available. Proactive librarians do more than just walk around the reference room muttering "There ought to be a index to these things"—they take action. The simplest step is to make suggestions to reference publishers. This can be done by letter or through conversations at conference exhibits. In recent years, reference publishers have had a new source of ideas, since they can monitor the professional e-mail groups and see what resources librarians need.

Many reference works (such as indexes to songs, fairy tales, and character names) came into being because librarians not only saw a particular need, but decided to take on the task themselves, either as a personal or an institutional project. Many reference books and databases began their life as a set of handwritten index cards in someone's desk drawer. These projects began as an attempt to capture and organize information to serve the needs of the staff and users at a single library, but as such homegrown tools prove their usefulness, librarians will realize that other libraries could benefit from access to what they have created.

Traditionally, librarians approached publishers to see if they were interested in a reference book based on their work. However, with the World Wide Web, librarians can now create valuable reference resources that are available to their own patrons (both within the library and remotely) and to other patrons around the world.

Web publishing is a natural for these reference projects. The noncommercial nature of Web publishing fits well with the mission of most libraries. Web publishing also allows for continual updating, an important benefit for indexes. Furthermore, Web publishing allows libraries to start with something basic and add new features as time and resources allow.

One such reference resource is the North Carolina Periodicals Index (*www.lib.ecu.edu/Periodicals/NCindex/ ncindex.html*), a project of the J. Y. Joyner Library of East Carolina University. Joyner Library maintains a North Carolina Collection, including many local and regional periodical titles. These periodicals included many articles valuable for research projects on the business, ecology, politics, and social issues of the region, but students were reluctant to use them because, in the words of Maurice C. York, "Most students would not take the time to look through back issues in the hope of finding pertinent information " (York, 1997).

The staff of Joyner Library decided to develop their own index to the regional periodicals, based on their own knowledge and experience of what would be most useful for their own students. The librarians selected which periodicals to include, and established the criteria for indexing. Because of staffing constraints, the project was designed to be as effective as possible, providing the maximum benefit for the time invested. The decision was made not to index reviews or articles less than a page in length, except when they would be particularly useful to students. The data-entry screens were designed to allow for quick and accurate data entry, and the PC-based database is periodically uploaded to the library Web server, where it is available to students at East Carolina University and elsewhere.

Since the development of this specialized indexing service, the regional periodicals are getting much more use by students. The time that the library invests in maintaining this resource is a good investment compared to the time librarians and students formerly spent trying to find needed information without an index (York, 1997).

## FORMAT VERSUS CONTENT

Very often the same information (or almost the same information) is now available to us in several different formats, each with advantages and disadvantages. Comparing these formats and making purchasing decisions can be very difficult.

Some of our patrons have marked preferences in terms of format—one group finds the computer a barrier to access and another finds the limitations of searching print a great burden in the electronic age. For some patrons, this is just a matter of personal preference, while for others there are special issues of accessibility. For example, full-text databases can be much easier for visually impaired patrons to use than print, as long as the appropriate adaptive technology is available.

Another factor is how many people can use the resource at the same time, a factor that can be limited by physical factors, network speed, and licensing agreements. Remote access is another issue—can people access the database from home? Also, the capabilities for searching, sorting, downloading, and printing can vary among different versions of the same product, and need to be taken into account.

It's important to know how often a product is updated. Generally, print updates are less frequent than CD-ROM updates (which are less frequent than online updates, but this can vary). Stability is another issue. Print has many limitations, but it's very stable. CD-ROMs are usually more stable than online resources, especially CD-ROMS on stand-alone, dedicated workstations. Networking within a building and beyond, and especially over the World Wide Web, adds many advantages in terms of currency and accessibility, but also adds complexity and sometimes stability problems. Every chain is only as strong as its weakest link, and increasingly there are many links in the chain between the user and the information.

Different versions of a product also require differing types and levels of software support. Locally mounted databases and CD-ROMs require some regular commitment of time to load updates, but generally reduce the support problems of telecommunications. PC-client versions of a product may require software loaded on individual workstations (which must be configured, updated, and maintained), while Web versions only require a standard browser on workstations. Web versions may bring their own control problems, since it may be difficult to secure PC workstations and limit access to browser options, or to limit some workstations to the reference databases only rather than to open Internet access.

Printing is a major issue—in fact, from reading the library-related e-mail lists, it seems that managing printing is one of the most troublesome problems of electronic reference services. The ability to print long lists of citations and the full text of articles seems to inspire patrons in a way that the microfilm reader/printer or the photocopy machine never did. Libraries can allow free printing, or charge for printing in a number of ways—including coin-operated printers, debit cards, centralized printing (with payment at pickup), and the honor system (with payment either at a public service desk or in some type of cash box). None of these methods is completely satisfactory to staff or patrons, and cost recovery is difficult.

Even more troublesome than charging for printing is the maintenance of printers—adding paper, unjamming paper, changing cartridges, and resolving networking problems. Even if there are computer support staff available for these tasks, the reference staff is inevitably the first line of support. The more full text that is available, the more patrons want to print.

## FULL-TEXT PERIODICALS DATABASES

For many decades, libraries subscribed to as many periodicals as they could afford, and devoted large amounts of space to long runs of periodicals, generally bound and limited to use within the library. Access to these periodicals collections was provided by the *Readers' Guide to Periodical Literature* and similar printed indexes. CD-ROM indexing products like InfoTrac were a major innovation, followed by the current wave of CD-ROM and online databases that include articles in full text.

Selecting among these products can be very difficult, and many questions must be asked. How full is full text? Are all articles included, or only articles of a certain length? What about book reviews, columns, brief news notes, and similar material? How many titles are available in full text, and how far back does the full text begin? Most databases include varying start dates for different titles. What is the vendor's policy on backfiles? Do they intend to retain the backfile indefinitely, or do they "cycle off" titles, only keeping the most recent five years of a title, for example, and dropping the older issues? What is their policy on adding and dropping titles from a database? What assurance do you have that such policies won't change?

Database quality can be difficult to evaluate without an intensive trial. Of course, vendors will be quick to point out any well-known titles that are exclusive to their product. Studying lists of titles broken down into subject areas can make it easier to identify the relative strengths and weaknesses of different databases. Large databases are likely to include many unfamiliar titles, which will vary in their usefulness. Some databases will include many regional publications and titles from outside the United States, which can be viewed as a strength or weakness. The best way to evaluate the databases is to try a series of searches on each and evaluate not only the interface, but also the quality of the results.

Another database issue is the quality of the abstracts and subject cataloging. The best way to evaluate these is to read several articles, preferably from different types of periodicals, and compare the abstracts and subject headings assigned by different vendors. Ideally, these articles would be from several disciplines, evaluated by librarians with subject expertise in those fields.

Spelling errors are also a database quality issue. Misspelled words not only reflect badly on the product and (by association) the library; they are also access issues for keyword searching. An easy way to check for spelling problems is to search for some commonly misspelled words, including some geographical and personal names.

There can be many complications over time with full-text databases. Sometimes vendors run into permission problems with individual articles within an issue. Sometimes the vendor loses the contract for a certain title, which may mean that the backfile for the title is also lost. You should understand how such changes are handled before you make decisions on dropping subscriptions or discarding back issues in print. Sometimes the vendor will fall behind on the indexing or full text for one or many titles. Other customers are your best source of information about this aspect of reliability. It's also helpful to search for a few subjects that have been in the news in the past month, which should help you evaluate how current the database is.

Of course, the interface and search capabilities of the database are of prime importance—it doesn't matter what sort of wonderful information is in the database if nobody can figure out how to find it. How easy is it to do a basic search, and what power options are included? Can a search be limited by date and length of article? Are proximity operators supported? What about natural-language searching? Can a search be limited to peer-reviewed journals? Is there an option to expand a search with a synonym list or fuzzy matching? Are these options easy to understand and use?

The output options should also be considered. What are the options for printing citations and articles? Is it possible to print only certain sections of an article? Can articles and citations be downloaded to a diskette? Can citations be imported in a bibliography management program? Can articles and citation lists be e-mailed?

It's also important to consider the balance between the articles that are available in full text and those that are not. Some products will allow you to enter your holdings information into your profile, so that articles can be tagged with a message if the periodical is available within the library. Searches can generally be limited to titles available in the library, to articles available in full text, or both. It seems that many patrons, however, find the availability of the full text online to be so convenient that they view the library's periodical collection as a last resort. Should the options be set so that searches are limited to full-text titles by default, since that's what most patrons seem to prefer, or should that option be off by default, to encourage greater use of the periodical collection?

The preference of students for using electronic full text almost exclusively can affect the quality of research. Since there is very little full text available from before 1990, relying on this format definitely limits any sort of historic perspective. Using full-text articles is also a different experience from using the actual periodicals. Seeing the periodical as a whole provides a better sense of context for the individual article. Even the advertisements reflect social and business history, and may be useful in providing clues about the times and the nature of the periodical's readership. Letters to the editor may offer corrections or substantive criticism of articles published in previous issues—sometimes with follow-up comments from the author. If these letters are excluded from the full text, does this accurately reflect the publication of the article in the periodical?

School and academic librarians sometimes feel conflict between the preferences of the students and the demands of the faculty. If students are relying too heavily on the full-text databases because they are easy to use, it is the responsibility of the teacher to require a broader style of research, although the librarian should certainly guide students toward the most appropriate resources, online or paper, and assist in their use.

### Books in Print

As libraries are seeking better ways of delivering access to traditional basic reference resources, the World Wide Web is changing the experiences and expectations of our patrons. For example, Bowker makes the *Books in Print* database available in print and on CD-ROM, and in various formats through other vendors, using the third-party vendor's interfaces. For many years, *Books in Print* was a unique and irreplaceable resource and the first stop for anyone who wanted to buy a book not readily available in bookstores.

Now, however, when online booksellers like Amazon. com (*www.amazon.com*) and Barnes and Noble (*www. barnesandnoble.com*) provide access to between two and three million titles, many of our patrons consider their catalogs a practical substitute for *Books in Print*. These catalogs have some added benefits (for example, users can interact with them, reading comments of other readers and adding their own), as well as many value-added features (including book recommendations and author interviews). They also, of course, do more than provide patrons with information about a book—they allow for instant ordering.

There are now also a number of sites including Bibliofind

(*www.bibliofind.com*) that provide access to the catalogs of independent used booksellers, as well as meta-sites like the Bookfinder (*www.bookfinder.com*) and Acses (*www.acses.com*), which send a single search to multiple online sellers of new and used books. The World Wide Web also lives up to its name, giving patrons access to booksellers outside the United States, including the British bookseller Bookstore.co.uk (*www.bookstore.co.uk*), which also supplies Spanish, Italian, French, and German books, and ships anywhere in the world.

However, as useful as these Web sites can be, is it wise for libraries to depend on the catalogs of such online vendors for such a basic reference resource? What assurance do we have that such catalogs will continue to be available? And is it ethical for libraries to point our patrons to these catalogs, whose *raison d'etre* is to sell books, and use them as reference resources?

*Books in Print* is not the only traditional reference source whose role is changing as the World Wide Web develops. *The Encyclopedia of Associations* is another example. Associations of all types and sizes now have their own Web sites, and searching directly for an association in a search directory such as Yahoo (*www.yahoo.com*) may be faster than looking it up in a book, and can get you directly to the Web site for the association itself rather than just provide a citation for it.

## OUTSIDE COMPETITION

Libraries are busy negotiating contracts to provide Web-based access to full-text newspaper and periodical databases to library users in our libraries and from home, school, and office. Meanwhile, we have competition from commercial services, which offer similar services directly to consumers, on either a subscription or pay-as-you-go basis.

Most large newspapers, for example, have their own Web sites, with searchable archives for the last several years. Typically searching is free, and retrieval of the full text costs somewhere from $1 to $4. Sometimes the citation alone is sufficient to answer a question, especially a date question. (When was the Hotel Vendôme fire? When did Senator Wilson resign?) Otherwise, anyone with a credit card can quickly get access to the full text of articles.

The Los Angeles Times (*www.latimes.com*) archives is typical of major metropolitan newspapers, with additional customized services available. There are also meta-sites like Newslibrary (*newslibrary.infi.net/*), which allow the user to search several newspapers simultaneously.

The Electric Library (*www.elibrary.com*), for example, provides access to a large collection of newspaper and periodical articles, radio and television transcripts, images, reference books, and other sources. Searches are entered in natural language, and a "best parts" feature jumps the user to the most relevant section of an article. The Electric Library has contracts with many school districts and public libraries, but is also promoted to home users on a subscription basis.

Northern Light (*www.northernlight.com*) is an interesting combination of an Internet search engine, not unlike HotBot, AltaVista, etc., and Special Collections, a large collection of full-text articles from general and special interest periodicals, newspapers, and reference books. By default, a search includes results from both the World Wide Web database and the Special Collections database. Users pay $1–$4 to retrieve the full text of Special Collections articles.

All of these services can be great for consumers, but they tend to encourage people to bypass the local public library. Someone in Southern California wanting an article from the *Los Angeles Times*, for example, may be aware that he could get this on microfilm at the local public library, but many people would be willing to pay a small charge to save a themselves a trip to the library, not to mention a session at the microfilm reader/printer. And the combination of Internet resources and articles from a service like Electric Library or Northern Light makes it possible for most students to do an adequate amount of research for many school projects at home, without ever visiting the library. This is a new situation that undercuts one of the public library's most important roles.

An increasing number of people have access to the Internet from home, school, or office, and many libraries have responded by licensing remote access to full-text databases for their patrons, using library card barcodes or similar means of validation. It's important for libraries to recognize the great value of home access to many library users, and to make sure that people in our communities are aware of the library alternative to the highly publicized commercial services. Such remote services should be promoted in traditional ways, including press releases and flyers distributed in the library, but they should also be promoted in ways that reach beyond current library users. Perhaps creative alliances can be made with local Internet Service Providers, for example, who can promote home access to full-text databases through the local library as a benefit of Internet access.

The library can also promote this service to teachers, who can encourage their students to use the library databases along with the general Web resources in doing their schoolwork. Many students think of the Internet as a substitute for using the library; they need help understanding that they can use the Internet to access valuable resources provided by the library.

Reference librarians can also promote value-added services for the home-accessible databases. Librarians can use e-mail to provide home users with the same help that they provide users at library workstations, suggesting subject headings and other search strategies, for example.

## UNPUBLISHED SOURCES

Sometimes the best answers are not from any published resource at all, but from subject experts who can interpret and respond directly to the patron's real question. Many reference librarians not only know where to look for information, they know who to call, and they know which method is apt to get the best answer. Sometimes they call a consulate, government office, or organization for answers. Many reference librarians also have developed a network of personal sources, including friends and relatives with special subject knowledge or experience who can provide useful background information or resources. In addition, libraries may have formal or informal arrangements with other libraries to provide backup reference services.

Many reference librarians have discovered the power of

e-mail groups and USENET newsgroups to get help with tough questions. STUMPERS is a popular e-mail group for posting tough reference questions, but there are also specialized subject groups on almost every imaginable (and some rather unimaginable) topics. Although there can be a concern for the authority of answers from these groups, it's often much easier to verify a particular answer than to find one. Sometimes you won't get the answer itself, but you will get a valuable clue that will lead you to the answer.

Many of the reference questions that we are asked are not new, even though they may be new to us. Searching the archives for STUMPERS will bring up many multiple answers for some popular reference questions, including the infamous "three words ending in *-gry*" and various commonly misattributed quotations. The STUMPERS archive is tricky to use, since you need to wade through the question, the clues, the definitive answer, and sometimes corrections to the definitive answer.

The FAQ (frequently asked questions) files associated with different USENET newsgroups are a wonderful resource. These questions were collected and answered because they came up frequently in the group, and most of the FAQ files have gone through a more intense peer review and revision process than any academic journal. Many of the FAQs have become the basis for their own Web sites—the much acclaimed Internet Movie Database (*www.imdb.com*) grew out of the FAQ files for rec.arts.movies—but most FAQs still also exist as plaintext files, posted to their groups on a regular basis to discourage newcomers from posting repeat questions. You can find hypertext versions of most FAQs at the Internet FAQ Consortium (*www.faqs.org/faqs/*).

Another way to get answers from USENET is to search the database of messages posted to thousands of different groups using Deja.com (*www.deja.com*). The chances are good that someone besides your patron wonders what that music is from the DeBeers diamond commercial, where to buy supplies for making Ukrainian Easter eggs, and whether large people can bring their own seat-belt extenders on an airplane.

If you can't find your answer in a FAQ or through a search, you can find an appropriate group and post the question. Unlike e-mail groups, you can browse through the different USENET groups, drop in and see current postings, and subscribe and unsubscribe from different groups, with no commitment or overflowing mailbox. In the world of USENET, to subscribe to a group just means to set a preference to view postings in the group. If you can find a group related your patron's question, you can post the question and tap the common knowledge of the group. If you do not have USENET access at work, you can still read and post messages through Deja.com's free personalized service.

## EVALUATION OF WEB RESOURCES

Librarians have expressed serious concerns about the accuracy and reliability of information on the World Wide Web and its use in a reference setting. The World Wide Web is a populist information utility, an open forum for communication of all types. Anyone can create Web pages with very little investment in time, effort, or expense. Free

Web-hosting services such as GeoCities and Tripod, along with public access to Internet workstations in libraries and elsewhere, have made it possible for people who don't own computers or know any HTML to participate fully in the World Wide Web.

The very openness of the World Wide Web is both its strength and its weakness. Librarians frequently mention that book publishers provide a filtering mechanism by only selecting books that pass certain standards of authority and quality, and that they add value through the editorial process by checking facts and editing text. However, the same editorial process also screens out material for commercial reasons—if a topic is not popular enough to guarantee sufficient sales, it will not be published. This different process thus eliminates a lot of material on rare medical conditions, unusual lifestyles, different points of view, odd hobbies, and other minority interests.

Librarians have a well-established practice for collection building: we read reviews, we select books that fill predictable needs, we catalog them and make them available to our users, and eventually we remove them from the collection. The World Wide Web resists our efforts to follow that process. Web sites change and grow, change location and contents and refuse to stay still while we review, select, and catalog them, and they have an unsettling habit of deselecting themselves by changing location or disappearing entirely.

Reference librarians have a particularly strained relationship with the World Wide Web, since some sites are similar to material that we are accustomed to working with in the reference environment, while others are much more similar to the circulating collection, popular magazines, and similar material that is generally beyond the scope of reference.

There have been many workshops, articles and, of course, Web pages on the topic of the evaluation of World Wide Web resources. The following six elements are frequently mentioned as criteria for evaluating Web sites:

- **Authority**: What is the source of the information? Who is responsible for the site, and what qualifications are listed? Is the site affiliated with a reputable organization in the field? Is there a statement describing the sponsorship and mission of the site, with contact information?
- **Accuracy**: Is factual material accurate? Is it clear what is fact and what is opinion?
- **Access**: Can the page be used by any browser, including a text browser, or is it dependent on tables, frames, graphics, Java, Shockwave, etc.? Is the site generally accessible? Do the pages load quickly? Does the page require registration? Are there fees associated with use of the site?
- **Currency**: Does the material seem to be current or is it outdated? Are there indications on the page of the frequency of updates? Do the individual pages have revision dates?
- **Presentation**: Is the material organized and presented in a clear and consistent manner? Are the navigation aids helpful? Can you easily search for a particular piece of information? Is the spelling and grammar acceptable?

- **Copyright:** Does the site appear to be in compliance with copyright guidelines?

Such checklists can be useful in selecting sites to be added to a library's Web page, for use in bibliographic instruction, and for helping patrons (especially students) evaluate the information that they find. Janet Alexander and Marsha Tate have developed a particularly useful set of World Wide Web evaluation resources for the Wolfgram Memorial Library of Widener University. They teach evaluation as one module in a multiphased approach to teaching World Wide Web research skills. Their evaluation resources (*www.science.widener.edu/~withers/webeval. htm*) include checklists for different types of Web pages (advocacy, business/marketing, news, informational, and personal), an approach that seems more helpful than generic lists of evaluative criteria. One particularly useful feature is their well-chosen collection of Web pages that can be used as examples of different issues.

Esther Grassian and Diane Zwemer have used these examples as the basis of a student exercise they created for the UCLA Library, called "Hoax? Scholarly research? Personal opinion? You decide!" (*www.library.ucla.edu/libraries/college/instruct/hoax/evlinfo.htm*). The UCLA team has also created an interactive quiz called "Whodunnit? What Kind of Web Page is This??" (*www.library.ucla.edu/libraries/college/instruct/environ/envindex.htm*) to test students' awareness of the issue of authorship or sponsorship of Web pages.

Although it is important for librarians to develop the skill and understanding to evaluate World Wide Web resources and to guide patrons, especially students, in their use, we also need to remember that it is the very open nature of it that makes the Web so interesting and useful to so many people. And from a reference viewpoint, Irene E. McDermott makes an interesting point:

> . . . we librarians spend so much time teaching critical thinking to our patrons to help them recognize unbiased Internet sites. But sometimes, they actually want one-sided information that they may not find on the shelf in your library. But they can get it, free and fast, on the open World Wide Web, along with information that refutes, amends, confirms, and even ridicules it (McDermott, 1998).

It is the glorious, unruly diversity that is the great richness of the World Wide Web: diversity of interest and opinion, and such a valuable supplement to the other, more traditional resources in our reference collections.

## FIVE STRATEGIES FOR SUCCESS

Reference collections are in a state of great change, as traditional print formats give way to various electronic formats, and as resources previously only found in libraries, like periodical indexes, are becoming directly available to home, office, and school users over the World Wide Web. Managing these changing resources can be difficult and challenging, but a collection of reference resources, on our shelves or electronically, is the foundation of reference service.

1. Think like a patron.
   Evaluate all collection decisions from the point of view
   of the patron. Are there works that people will want
   to borrow to use at home? Is there a way that you
   can make that happen?

2. Weigh all the factors when choosing among formats.
   When faced with a decision between formats, consider
   all of the pros and cons of each format: physical space,
   ease of use, number of simultaneous users, access from
   the library and remotely, and so forth. Make lists, discuss the options with colleagues, and make a decision.

3. Consider the infrastructure.
   Make sure that you consider the relationship between
   collection decisions and the physical infrastructure that
   supports your services. Print resources require adequate shelving, tables, and chairs to support their use;
   electronic resources require adequate workstations in
   the library; and remote use of electronic resources requires an adequate networking arrangements.

4. Build in some redundancy.
   To make the most effective use of limited financial resources, the majority of our collection decisions involve choosing one resource over another, trying to
   get as wide a variety of information as possible. However, in certain core areas, you want to build in some
   redundancy. For example, most libraries find basic at-
   lases, almanacs, dictionaries, and popular encyclopedias still getting heavy use. These resources serve as a
   backup system to electronic resources at times when

all workstations are in use or out of service, and they are also used by patrons who need a quick fact or who are not yet comfortable using electronic alternatives.

5. Evaluate all areas of the reference collection.
   So much has changed, and we need to examine all areas of our collection to make sure that they are still worth the time and money that we invest to maintain them. Vertical files, college catalogs, company annual reports, and telephone books are all special collections that have been maintained by many reference departments. These special collections are often expensive to maintain in terms of staff time, and they also sometimes occupy a considerable amount of space. The value of these collections needs to be reexamined now that much of this information is available on the World Wide Web.

Our library users deserve the best collections that we can arrange for their use, whether those collections are used in our libraries or from home. Collection management has gotten far more complicated over the last ten years, but the variety, amount, and quality of information available through most libraries has increased dramatically through the World Wide Web and licensed proprietary databases.

# Chapter 5

# Time and Space

In most libraries, reference is not only a set of services; it is also a place—a whole floor, a room, or at least a special area. In most libraries, the place called reference is anchored by the reference desk. The layout and design of the reference department play a major role in defining the nature of the reference services that will be offered by the library.

In smaller libraries, including many school and special libraries as well as small public libraries, there is usually only one service point and often only one librarian. Reference services are offered, and they may in fact be the predominant services in some small libraries, but they are not *separate* services. Librarians in small libraries offer circulation and reference services, along with interlibrary loan, technical support, and general help, in an integrated, holistic way. It's only when a library reaches a certain size and level of staffing that we begin to see specialization—circulation over here, reference over there.

Integrated services can be offered at a very high level, as they often are in small, special libraries, and have one major benefit to both the librarian and the library user: directness. The patron never has to find the right desk and launch into a reference encounter "cold." The librarian never has to refer the patron to another service point. And in most small libraries, the librarian and library users know each other, making reference an ongoing service rather than a series of brief encounters. After starting work together on a reference project, either partner in the venture can contact the other a day later to say, "I thought of something else that might help . . . ."

In fact, much of professional practice in larger libraries is really designed to try to compensate for the loss of the sense of context that is natural in small libraries. We perform a reference interview to try to understand the question because we do not have an ongoing relationship with most of our patrons. We ask if we have completely answered their questions, because most of our encounters take place in an atmosphere of anonymity, and we need closure because we don't usually have the opportunity to follow up after the fact.

Although small libraries can offer an unmatched level of personal service, most public and academic libraries, and many school and special libraries, are of a size where some level of specialization is practiced, both in terms of the layout of the library itself and in staffing. The way that space and staff are distributed reflects the way that we think of reference, and will affect the way that our library users think about and use these services.

## THE REFERENCE AREA

The first question to be decided about the reference room is whether it should be a room at all, or whether it should be an open area within the building. The problem with an enclosed area is that it is visually separated from the rest of the building, and tends to be intimidating to patrons and isolating to staff. The problem with an open area is that it tends to lose its identity and both staff and services tend to merge with general library activity.

Many modern libraries have a reference area that combines the benefits of both approaches: one that is not totally enclosed by walls, but that has boundaries defined by architecture and furnishings. The most important issue is really whether all library users have sufficient visual cues to lead them to the reference area, or if it is hidden away in the building, approached only by those in the know.

The reference area presents an inherent design conflict because of the nature of the activities that we expect to take place there. Most libraries use the room to serve two major functions: as a place for patrons to use reference material and as a place for librarians to provide answers, instruction, and assistance to patrons. The first activity implies a need for quiet, and the second brings with it a certain level of noise.

In fact, reference areas have gotten noisier over the past several years. The increased emphasis on doing a proper reference interview and understanding the importance of not just answering the patron's initial question means that most librarians are spending longer in productive conversation with each patron. The increasing complexity of electronic resources means that we have greatly expanded resources to offer our patrons, but that we must spend more time instructing them in their use—another source of noise, even when the PCs themselves aren't beeping, playing music, or emitting other interesting sounds.

Another source of increased sound in the reference room is the result of a move at all levels of education—kindergarten to graduate school—from individual work to group projects. When tables of four students are engaged in a lively conversation in the reference room today, it is probably not because they are socializing and neglecting their assignments, as was often the case in the past, but because they are doing their work—together, as assigned.

One response to these changes in the nature and sound level of reference services has been to add designated quiet study rooms somewhere near the reference room, which itself used to be the quiet study room for the library. This can be a large, traditional study room with tables or carrels, or smaller, glass-enclosed cubicles for one or two people. Some libraries offer both individual study rooms and one or more small-group study rooms. It's an interesting combination of approaches: small rooms offer quiet people refuge from the sounds of a busy reference room, and offer study groups a place to talk without adding to that noise.

One situation to consider is the needs of tutoring groups. Many libraries offer formal or informal literacy and English as a Second Language (ESL) programs, often with the use of volunteer tutors. Other libraries offer some level of support to outside organizations that provide this type of service. In addition, other students work individually with tutors for remedial help with schoolwork. The library offers an appropriate atmosphere for such work, but tutoring often involves almost steady talking, which can be disturbing to others, and working in public can be inhibiting to the student. Small study rooms are ideal for tutoring and ESL sessions.

In addition to separate quiet study rooms and smaller, glass enclosed individual and group study rooms, libraries can provide a balance of quieter and noisier places within the building. There may be quieter areas of the library that are outside of the reference room, but not too remote, where scattered seating can be used to create additional study space. It's helpful to have different types of seating: traditional tables for general study, study carrels for privacy and concentration, and comfortable seating for reading.

Dispersed seating and study areas around the building provide an atmosphere where patrons can usually find something that suits their individual needs on any particular visit. However, with seating and study areas dispersed around the building, or even in different parts of the reference room itself, there is an increased burden on the library staff who need to monitor those areas both for the security of patrons, facilities, and materials, and to offer assistance. Building layouts need to be planned with staffing levels in mind—and thereafter, staffing levels need to be planned with the building layout in mind.

## THE REFERENCE DESK

Much has been written over the last several years on reinventing reference, tiered reference services, deskless reference, roving reference, and other alternatives to the traditional image of the reference librarian passively seated at the reference desk, waiting to be approached.

Some libraries have abolished the reference desk, or merged it with circulation into a single service point. Others have supplemented the traditional reference desk with an information desk, designed to handle procedural and directional questions, freeing the staff at the reference desk for more complex questions. Some have separate reference and reader's advisory desks, while others have separate reference desks in different subject areas or parts of the building.

Through all the possible configurations, the one thing that remains constant is the fact that the primary role of the reference librarian is the one that defined the profession in the beginning: giving personal assistance to the library user. In order to give assistance, the librarian and the user must come together. The reference desk serves the same function that information desks serve in stores, airports, and other public places—that of providing an identifiable contact zone, a place where people know they can request help.

### Height of the Reference Desk

Perhaps the most important question about the design of the primary reference service point is its height. Is it low, the same height as a standard office desk, designed for staff to be seated in chairs? Or is it counter height, designed for staff to be standing or perhaps sitting on high stools? The question is suprisingly controversial, and experienced, professional reference librarians have serious disagreements over which is preferable for service.

In discussions on LIBREF-L, for example, R. Lee Hadden wrote:

> High desks are used in police stations to intimidate, and to turn applicants into supplicants. High desks are also used in courtrooms to make doddering fools look impressive. If this is how your library management sees the library patrons and staff, then you have more problems than just a disagreement over high desks.

Laura K. Brendon of the Eisenhower National Clearing-house for Mathematics and Science Education, agrees:

> Several people have mentioned images of power that high desks conjure (they also remind me of banks and department stores—"we need to defend our merchandise/money against marauders"). In my observation, far more people apologized for "bothering" me with a reference question when I was behind this type of desk than when I'm at a normal height desk. It's true that a tall desk is easier to work at when standing, but I'll gladly trade the discomfort involved in rising to help people with the image of more approachability . . . .

However, others feel that patrons find the counter-height service desks to be more approachable. Jay Evatt, of the University of Georgia Libraries, writes, "The most obvious benefit is that a high reference desk places the reference librarian at eye level with the people on the other side of the desk. Being at eye level with the user facilitates both nonverbal and verbal communication."

Some librarians report experience in situations where two desks, high and low, were available, and noted that patrons had a marked preference for the high desk. Susan E. Thomas of Valdosta State College writes, "In one library we had both a counter high service desk and a regular desk connected together. Even when only the regular desk was staffed, patrons would still stop at the counter high desk and stand there staring at the librarian at the regular desk."

Bob Boyce notes, "At Lincoln City Libraries we have had a 'higher' reference desk for several years. Before that we had a combination, with two stations higher and one at normal desk height. People *always* avoided the normal height desk and would stand in line at the higher desk, even when no one was being helped at the normal desk!"

These experiences echo those reported many years ago, in one of the few articles in the professional literature on this topic. In her article, "Patron Preferences in Reference Service Points," Linda Morgan reports on her informal study observing patrons at the M.D. Anderson Library of the University of Houston. She noted a marked preference for approaching the counter-height service point, and writes that many patrons would wait for service from the librarian at the counter, even when the librarian at the low desk was not with a patron (Morgan, 1980).

An earlier article written by Robert Pierson in 1977 noted a trend at that time away from counter-height reference desks, and suggests that reference librarians felt that lower desks distinguished them from the more transactional, clerical activities of the circulation desk, and even the desire to dissociate themselves from "shopclerks and bartenders." However, it seems clear that the public has been conditioned by their experiences in other public settings like stores, banks, airports, and hotels, to seek help from personnel standing at counters (Pierson, 1997).

Whatever the height of the desk, however, it is the attitudes and actions of the staff that determine the quality of service. In a message to LIBREF-L, Catherine Cox of the University of San Francisco writes, "The height of the reference desk makes less difference than my willingness to get out from behind the desk completely," and notes, "When I am out from behind the desk, I may be approached by five or six different people before I ever get back to my chair."

The most successful desk is probably one that combines both a high area that serves as an obvious, approachable place to seek help, and a lower area where both staff and patrons can be seated for a few minutes, and which can serve as a comfortable point for working with children, short adults, and patrons or staff who are in wheelchairs or who have other conditions that make standing uncomfortable.

Reference service can vary from brief, directional, and ready-reference questions to lengthy consultations. The physical setting of the reference department, including the reference desk, should encourage flexibility and movement.

## BEYOND THE DESK

The reference desk, however it is configured, is the primary point of contact for library users who have consciously decided that they need help from a librarian. They may have a specific question they want answered or they may want some guidance finding the best sources for a particular project. They may have entered the building with the intention of going to reference to ask for assistance or they may have tried to find what they needed and then decided to ask for help.

These people who approach the desk and ask a question are the official, self-declared reference patrons, but they are not the only ones in the library on any given day who need our assistance. Some patrons will not approach the reference desk for service—we need to find them and offer assistance.

### Roving Reference

In addition to assigning reference librarians to cover the reference desk, some libraries assign librarians to perform roving reference—to walk around the library offering assistance to patrons. Some of the people they approach don't choose to accept assistance, but at least they have been reminded that librarians are available to assist them when they do. Others welcome the help. They may be physically lost (in the wrong section of the stacks, for example) or perhaps just not finding what they need.

If these patrons need assistance, why don't they just approach the reference desk and ask for help? There are many answers to this question. Some people may not even know that there is a reference desk where help is available. Some would eventually give up and ask for help, but haven't quite reached that point yet. Others just don't like to ask for help, because they are shy or perhaps because they feel like they ought to be able to use the library independently. This can be a negative side effect from years of library instruction in school: some students get the message that they are supposed to master library and skills and not have to get help from a librarian.

Another factor can be the atmosphere in a busy reference room. Many patrons find it intimidating to ask personal, self-revealing questions where they can be overheard by other patrons waiting in the queue or working nearby. These personal questions may be about confidential legal or medical matters, but patrons may also feel inhibited about asking many other types of questions, including "stupid" ones. Approached in another part of the building, where there may be fewer people around to overhear, some patrons are much more willing to explain what they need.

Even if librarians are not actually assigned to roving reference, many make it a practice to approach patrons as they walk around the library in the normal course of their library duties. Some librarians approach almost everyone they see; most offer assistance to anyone who looks like he or she might need some help. Some librarians have more of a problem with this proactive aspect of reference, and they need to be encouraged to approach patrons to offer help.

One special form of roving reference is to check up on patrons who have previously been helped in reference and have spent a little time working on their own. This follow-up provides an opportunity to confirm that patrons are finding what they need or to suggest a different approach. For reference encounters that do not end with an answer to a question, but instead with the reference librarian guiding the patron toward sources that should be helpful, there can really be no closure without this type of follow-up.

### Technical Assistance

Patrons using electronic resources often find themselves needing help. They may have technical problems like printer jams, have questions about the use of a particular program, or need assistance with search terms or interpreting results. The user in such cases needs help, but can't abandon the workstation and go to the reference desk for assistance. Reference librarians need to monitor all workstations for potential problems, which is not always easy as the number of workstations increases. What's really needed is an easy way for patrons to indicate that they need help that doesn't require them to leave their workstation, perhaps something like the call buttons on airplanes or the flashing lights at supermarket cashier stations.

## OTHER REFERENCE SERVICES

Although we tend to think of reference primarily in terms of providing instant, on-demand assistance to library users, there are other reference services that also need appropriate places, staffing, and scheduling.

### Research Consultation

Many of our patrons come to the library with a situation that is more complex than just a single reference question. A professor may be planning a new course, an entrepreneur may be considering a new business venture, and a student may be considering a particular topic for a major independent study project. A skillful reference interview may elicit one particular question, but the way most of us do reference—standing in the middle of a crowded reference room, with the phone ringing and other patrons waiting for service—does not really provide an appropriate setting for the sort of professional consultation that would be really helpful.

The typical reference setup, with people waiting in line for service, makes a longer consultation awkward for both patron and librarian. In a bank, you wait in line to see a teller, with whom you might have a brief conversation as you ask a couple of questions about your account, but if you want to apply for a mortgage, you probably want to sit down somewhere else with a loan officer and have his or her undivided attention for ten or 15 minutes to go over your options.

A reference consultation is very similar. A librarian and a patron sit down together, in a room that is not open to the public. This is important for ensuring privacy and concentration. The room can be an office or a consultation room similar to those found in banks and other offices, furnished with a table and chairs. Ideally, it should have some basic reference resources in it, including a workstation, but this isn't absolutely necessary. The purpose of the consultation is not to answer the patron's questions, but to hear about the project and what information is needed, and to develop some approaches to finding what the patron needs. At the end of the session, the librarian should clearly restate what has been decided and what will happen next. This might include assignments for both the patron and the librarian—for example, it might be agreed that the patron will begin looking for books and articles on the topic, with some guidance from the librarian, while the librarian takes ownership of a few factual questions and promises to report back to the patron in a specified amount of time with the results.

In many libraries, reference librarians arrange to be off the desk and to sit down in an office for all sorts of other consultations—with sales representatives, consultants, and other staff members—but not with patrons. Some feel that such consultations are beyond the scope of reference, and that they result in a few patrons getting too much attention, at the expense of others. However, the consultation can be a very efficient method of performing reference, and can save time for both the patron and librarian. The setting resembles that of professional consultations that people have with doctors, lawyers, and accountants. Once both parties are sitting down in a quiet environment, patrons often find it much easier to express their information needs, with minimal prompting from the librarian.

Even if no special room is designated as a reference consultation room, reference librarians can sit down with patrons in an office or group study room. The consultation session may grow out of a traditional reference encounter: when it becomes clear that the patron has something more than a simple question, the librarian can suggest that they sit down together, saying something like, "so you can tell me more about your project and how I can help you find what you need."

Patrons can also be encouraged to make an appointment for a reference consultation. Reference librarians spend an increasing amount of time booking other resources, like Internet workstations and group study rooms, but perhaps the most useful resource we can book is ourselves. Encouraging patrons to make an appointment for a consultation helps people get organized before they arrive, and enables the library to plan appropriate staffing.

In an academic or school library, reference consultations are used by both faculty and students. Faculty may be planning a new course, changing a current course, or preparing an assignment and looking into what resources will be available to support their students; or they might be working on their own research projects. Students can benefit from a personal consultation as they plan major independent study projects or term papers. A consultation session before the student plunges into research can save both the student and the library time in the long run.

In a public library, consultation sessions may also be requested by students and teachers, by local business people planning a new venture, jobseekers, or by anybody with a personal situation or project that presents a set of information needs. For example, a parent whose child has just been diagnosed with a learning disability may need general information on the disability, referrals to local support services, or citations from relevant state law.

Whether or not a library wants to offer a formal reference consultation service, all libraries deal with a wide range of reference interactions, from directional questions to simple fact-checking questions to more complex questions requiring a full reference interview to situations best handled by the reference consultation. The distinctions between the full reference interview and the reference consultation service may be subtle. A few distinguishing characteristics of the reference consultation service are that both parties are seated (which is a physical symbol that says "you have my full attention"), notes are taken by the librarian (and often by the patron), and names and contact information are exchanged for later follow-up.

### Bibliographic Instruction

Academic and school libraries have a long history of bibliographic instruction. These libraries often offer both a formal program of general library instruction as well as special sessions for individual classes. Public libraries, especially children's and young adult services departments, have also traditionally done some bibliographic instruction, generally in conjunction with the schools, and usually in the form of a library tour or class visit.

In the 1980s when online public access catalogs were introduced, many public libraries found that patrons had trouble understanding concepts like subject headings and keyword searching, and needed more help than it was possible to give them as they were trying to perform a particular search. For many patrons, the online public access catalog was the first database searching program that they had ever used, and for some it was their first experience using any type of computer. Many libraries responded by offering introductory online catalog sessions for small groups of people.

As more and more electronic resources have been added to library collections, and especially with the great rush of interest in the Internet that began in the early 1990s, many libraries of all types expanded their bibliographic instruction. Many public libraries now offer introductory sessions and special searching sessions on high-interest topics (like job searching or genealogy), or for particular groups of users (like senior citizens).

One problem in offering these sessions has been trying to provide hands-on experience at workstations that are laid out for general reference use rather than for group instruction. As these sessions have become an increasingly important service in all types of libraries, many have responded by designing electronic classroom space for both staff and public training sessions.

## STAFFING

Reference librarians and the support staff assigned to the reference department have many tasks to perform, all of which require an appropriate allocation of time and space.

### *On-Desk/Off-Desk Time*

Reference librarians and their assistants are engaged in an endless balancing act between background duties (including collection development, planning, budgeting, scheduling, training, and committee work), and the primary role of providing direct service to library users. Direct service always takes precedence, since it is generally provided on demand, while other tasks can be shifted in time, to some extent. The problem is that many reference librarians find that they have insufficient time for these important professional background tasks, especially in times of heavy demand, staff shortages, and other constraints.

In most libraries, reference librarians are assigned specific times when they are responsible for public service, and other hours when they are not. This plan ensures that some amount of time is reserved for other duties; it works best when reference librarians have a workspace far enough away from the public service area to avoid the distractions of that environment. Off-desk time not only provides time for other duties, it also improves the quality of reference

service by keeping librarians from doing too many con-
secutive hours of public service. Most librarians find that
their ability to focus and provide optimal service declines
after a two- to four-hour shift in a busy reference room.

In other libraries, especially smaller ones, there is no designated off-desk time, and reference librarians, are responsible for covering public service for almost all of their
working hours, with other tasks performed during slow
periods on the desk. This arrangement presents a very basic public service problem: staff members who are performing other tasks between patrons look busy, and patrons
are reluctant to disturb them with questions. Some staff
members have a tendency to "set up shop" on the reference desk, and to become engrossed in their work, rather
than proactively offering assistance to patrons in the area.

In some libraries, it may not be possible to eliminate the
practice of having staff members performing other work
while covering a public service desk, but this practice needs
to be examined and controlled to ensure that the quality
of public service does not suffer. One of the best ways to
do this is to follow the basic principles of time management and other forms of budgeting. Reference librarians
need to keep an accounting of the various tasks for which
they are responsible, prioritize them, and decide how much
staff time can be allotted to each. When a new assignment
or service arrives, staff need to estimate how much time
this will require, and then decide where that time will come
from. If serving on a committee will consume two hours
a week, where will those two hours come from?

## WHEN DOES REFERENCE HAPPEN?

We have been talking about space—the physical layout of the library and where reference services occur—but we also need to think about time, and when reference services are offered.

For many libraries, the answer is simply, "all hours that the library is open." This is generally true for smaller libraries, where there is no separate reference department or staff—if the library is open, whoever is working will assist patrons with any type of question, whether it is related to circulation, reader's advisory services, or reference.

In larger libraries, where there is a separate reference room and reference staff, the goal is usually to provide services during all hours that the library is open. In some libraries, the reference desk is always staffed by professional librarians who are members of the reference department. In other libraries, there are times when the reference desk may be covered by paraprofessionals, or by librarians from other departments. Some libraries have hours, typically late evening or weekend hours, when the library is open but full reference service is not offered.

There are many benefits to having staff members from other departments spend some time working in the reference department. Administrators, technical services librarians, and children's librarians who cover reference will have a better understanding of reference issues. Administrators who cover reference may be more understanding of training and staffing issues in that department; technical services librarians gain valuable insight into cataloging seen from the user's side; and children's librarians, who are often the first professional contact point for parents and teachers as well as younger students, will have a better understanding of what resources are available in reference.

However, when many different people are involved in covering reference, it's important to provide training, supervision and evaluation for all, and to provide channels of communication so that changes in resources, practices, and procedures are known to all. These needs are not new, but in recent years, with the rapid pace of change in the reference department, the needs have become more acute. The problems of coordinating training, communication, and evaluation are made more complex when dealing with a diverse staff, which includes both members of the reference staff and members of other departments, full-time and part-time staff, and professionals and paraprofessionals.

There is also an inherent problem of supervision here. The reference librarian is responsible for the quality of service offered, but may not be the supervisor of many of the people who are providing that service. In fact, sometimes the supervisor of the reference librarian is one of the people covering some hours of reference service.

The more people who cover reference, the more important it is to develop a system that ensures that all staff members covering reference receive some regular training and have a regular system of communication in place. This is especially true in libraries with high staff turnover, many part-time and weekend staff members, or staff members from other departments covering reference. It's much better to set aside time to provide people with the information that they need to do a good job in reference than it is to deal with the problems and hard feelings caused by inadequately trained staff or by people who are out of the communication loop.

Sometimes librarians are so busy managing information for our patrons that we don't devote enough attention to communicating information to other staff members—perhaps we are like the shoemaker's children who go barefoot. Whether we use notebooks, bulletin boards, e-mail, meetings, training sessions, or some combination of these, it's important for all staff members covering reference service to feel that they have the information and skills they need to handle most situations. When these systems break down, you will hear frequent cries of "Well, nobody ever told me . . . ." and "How was I supposed to know that?" It's also important that all staff members understand the importance of referring anything that they can't handle to another staff member, even if that means taking down the patron's name and phone number for follow-up the next day.

## EXTENDED SERVICES

We have been speaking of traditional reference services, in which we have both a reference space (the library building) and a reference time (hours that we are in that building) and the patron must approach us within that space and time. Telephone reference service was the first major extension, since it allowed patrons to use our services without actually coming to the building. Electronic services, however, greatly extend our reference services beyond the traditional limits of space and time.

## Remote Access for Patrons

Many libraries now offer patrons access to some number of services from home, school, or office. These services may be direct dial-in services, but increasingly they are offered over the Internet. Access to the library catalog is the most basic service that libraries offer, but many libraries also offer access to other high-quality reference databases (including full-text periodicals databases, online encyclopedias, and other products); usually access is limited to the library's cardholders (with validation by the patron's library barcode, student identification number, or some similar system).

As more and more patrons have home access to the Internet, these services become increasingly important. With high-quality, licensed reference databases, the library is adding an important element of content that supplements freely available World Wide Web resources. Providing remote access to these databases is a great convenience to patrons, extends our services to 24 hours a day, and relieves some of the demand for library workstations.

If we offer remote access to resources, however, we have to support it, which can be complicated. There are many frustrating problems with connecting, validations, screen displays, and printing that are difficult to diagnose, since they may involve problems with the patron's equipment and configurations, the patron's Internet Service Provider, the local system, the database vendor, or some combination of these. Although providing technical support to remote users is probably not the job of reference librarians, they are often the ones who hear about these problems, and they must provide basic help and referrals.

Reference librarians are often uniquely qualified to provide a first line of technical support, since through training and experience they know how to get beyond the initial statement of the problem and get the information needed for troubleshooting. Because of these skills, even in situations where systems staff are providing technical support for library users, reference librarians should be involved in developing training material, FAQ files, and other supporting material for the remote users of library reference systems.

### Distance Education

Academic libraries are increasingly supporting distance learning programs. Students may be pursuing credits, certificates, or degrees based wholly or in part on work that takes place off campus. Libraries supporting distance learning programs use a combination of methods, including providing access to appropriate licensed databases and offering reference support through a combination of telephone service (often using toll-free numbers), fax, and e-mail. Some libraries are experimenting with a variety of other techniques, including conferencing and messaging technologies, which allow for a reference interview to take place online in real time, sometimes with the ability to have patron and librarian looking at screens for online help and instruction using electronic databases. In fact, the new technologies used to support distance learning can also be used to benefit other library users who need reference services but who cannot or prefer not to come to the library.

## FOUR STRATEGIES FOR SUCCESS

We are living in a very complex time for librarianship. Traditional reference services are still practiced, used, and valued, while the World Wide Web continues to change the world of information, making it possible for the average person to have direct access to an array of public and private resources that could hardly have been imagined just ten years ago.

1. See ourselves as others see us.
   We become so familiar with our own libraries that it is hard to experience them the way our users do, especially new users, but we can try. Walk into the library through all entrances used by the public, and look around. If you needed help, how would you know where to go, and who to ask? Walk around to different parts of the library and ask yourself the same question. Have several staff people try this and compare results.

   The real test, though, is to find people who have never been to your library before and ask them to do the same thing. Be sure to include people who aren't experienced library users. How did they find someone who could help them, and how long did it take them?

2. Keep the reference staff available and approachable.
   High desk, low desk, or no desk—the more important issue from the library users' point of view is that they connect with staff members who will provide friendly, competent service. The reference desk can be a convenient place for users to find help, but many

people find it awkward to approach the desk, whatever its design, unless librarians make an effort to welcome them, and are willing to move out from behind the desk to help them.

Many visitors to your library will need help but will never approach, or even find, the reference desk. Encourage all staff members to approach library patrons and offer assistance, and encourage circulation staff to ask people checking out material if they found everything they were seeking.

3. Balance the interests of patrons in and out of the building.

Most of us are most comfortable serving people who come to the library and approach the reference desk. However, we need to respect the needs and choices of those who access our services from their homes or offices, whether by telephone, e-mail, fax, or some other method. Develop policies and procedures that balance the needs of all users, and give everyone equal time and service, whether they walk into your building or use the telephone or e-mail.

4. Have a plan to support users at computer workstations.

As more and more of our resources move from print to computer workstations, you need a plan to support that group of users. Who is responsible for booking time at the workstations or enforcing time limits? Who is responsible for technical support? Who is responsible for reference support—helping users find the kind of information that they need?

Many libraries that successfully handled these matters informally when they had two or three CD-ROM workstations are overwhelmed now that they have far more workstations, providing a complex array of resources. Effective support requires planning and appropriate staffing, which may include experimenting with some creative options. These plans need to be worked out with the full cooperation of the library administration, and evaluated and adapted as circumstances change—and they will change.

We need to move beyond defining reference in terms of just the activity that centers around the reference desk, and concentrate on looking at ways that our core value of providing personal service to users can be extended. New technologies make it possible for us to be giving service at hours when our building is closed, and to have library users who never come near our library building.

# Chapter 6

# Questions, In and Out

Many people come to the library looking for various kinds of information. They want to know about Russian history or French cooking or Japanese architecture. They want to know how to crochet an afghan or build a deck or write poetry. They find books and other material on all of these topics by using the catalog or browsing book displays. Many readers have a few nonfiction areas that they browse on a regular basis.

Most of the time readers use the nonfiction collections of the library with a minimum of assistance. They are interested in exploring a particular subject, seeking knowledge rather than the answer to a specific question. However, there are times when our patrons are not interested in reading a whole book to increase their general understanding of some topic, but they need a specific piece of information. A question is the expression of this need for information, and reference librarians help people find the answers to their questions by referring to books and other sources of information.

Sometimes a reference question is just a matter of curiosity. A person calls the library or comes to the reference desk because he wants to know where the expression "a pig in a poke" comes from. No reason—he's just wondering. Maybe it's come up in conversation recently. Sometimes reference questions arise because people are pursuing some larger goal and find that they need some particular piece of information. One person is preparing a speech and needs to confirm the source of a quotation. Another is planning a party with a Mardi Gras theme and needs a recipe for King's Cake. In other cases, the patron is dealing with a major project and needs help finding and using various sources of information. The research project could be academic, like a term paper, or personal, like searching for a new career or coping with a health problem.

Most people satisfy most of their information needs on their own, or with the help of various other people: friends, teachers, doctors, lawyers, and so on. But when they have questions that fall through the cracks, or that they want to research on their own but need a little help, they turn to the library and the help of reference librarians.

## TYPES OF QUESTIONS

It may be helpful to look at some of the types of reference questions that patrons ask, and to look at the different issues related to each type of question.

### Questions with Answers

Factual questions are perhaps the most common type of reference question, or at least the one that we most commonly have in mind when discussing the reference question. The patron is looking for a single, identifiable piece of information that presumably exists. What's the state bird of Delaware, the capital of Florida, the national anthem of Israel? Who said, "Success is counted sweetest by those who ne'er succeed?" What is the literacy rate of Mali? Can I plug in my hairdryer in Costa Rica without an adapter? What's the address of the professional association for occupational therapists? Who's the head of state of Brazil? How many moons does Saturn have? Who are my representatives in Congress?

The patron just wants a fact: a name, an address, a number. The important issues for these questions are speed and accuracy. These are the questions that we need to dispatch quickly, to satisfy the patron and to allow time for patrons who need more extensive help.

There are many pitfalls, however, with these deceptively simple questions. Sometimes they do not have an answer. This is often the case for statistical questions—the question sounds simple, but you can't find any study that provides an answer. For example, the question may be "What percentage of full-time college students are over the age of 30?" An interesting question, and one that certainly has an answer, but if nobody has counted recently, the answer may not be known.

There is also the problem of giving inaccurate information from presumably authoritative sources. Even reference books have errors in them, and once misinformation gets into print, the error is often replicated in other sources. It's good practice to verify an answer in a second source, but in practice, very few librarians have time to do this for every question, and seldom do so for simple questions.

Another problem is that the answer may have changed since the source was published. The president of Brazil may have died or left office in the last few weeks, and you may not have noticed this in the news. Delaware may have voted in a new state bird, or astronomers may have discovered a new moon of Saturn. How do we verify that the information that we have is still true?

This used to be a difficult problem, and many libraries developed systems to maintain current information. Some created information sheets of federal, state, and local government officials, which were updated as needed, and they relied on these resources rather than any printed source. Some libraries had systems of designating certain reference books as the first source to be used for certain types of questions, flagging entries to alert staff members to look for updates in a clipping file.

These systems were reasonably effective in updating information, but were time-consuming to maintain. Electronic resources, including both periodical databases and the World Wide Web, have greatly improved the ability of libraries to get current information without maintaining their own files. Paper reference sources can only be updated by the printing and distribution of new editions or updates, but electronic sources can be updated instantly. Reference librarians in search of current information now rely on authoritative, official Web pages (for example, those of government departments and agencies), and can go one step further and search periodicals and news databases for any new developments.

### Information Requests

Sometimes the patron asks for information about a subject, not the single answer to a question. What the patron expects is to receive something roughly equivalent to an encyclopedia article—a few paragraphs that define or explain or otherwise satisfy a need for information about something. What is the origin of the Jack O'Lantern? What was the Boston Molasses Flood? Who was Mary McLeod Bethune? Why do Amish dolls have no faces?

The same issues of accuracy apply here, but the patron is looking for information that is a little more extensive than a simple fact. The important issue here is completeness, making sure that the answer you provide is sufficient for the patron's purpose. For example, is it enough to give the patron the date and bare statistical facts of the Molasses Flood, without pointing to more accounts of this bizarre and fascinating disaster? Is the following a sufficient answer to the Mary McLeod Bethune question: "1875–1955, African-American educator, Presidential adviser, and founder of the National Council of Negro Women"? It's possible, but unlikely, that that's all the patron needs to know.

### Pointers

Sometimes the patron is going to write a paper or begin some piece of independent research, and needs help getting started. The patron may begin with a specific question, but really needs you to show him or her what resources you have available and how to use them.

The important issue here is communication. The librarian and patron need to work together to make sure that both the nature of the research and the use of resources are understood. For any sort of extensive research, the patron is likely to be using some combination of books from the circulating and reference collections, periodicals databases, Internet resources, and other CD-ROM or online databases. To work successfully through all of these different types of resources, the patron is likely to need help now and then, and should always be encouraged to come back for more help. Checking up on a patron who has been sent to the stacks or to a workstation to see how he or she is doing and to offer additional help is also an effective technique.

### Tricksters

These are the tricky ones—the "Who am I?" questions, the "three words ending in -*gry*," contrived questions, brainteasers, and science puzzlers. Which freezes first, hot water or cold water? Does water go down the drain in a different direction in the Southern hemisphere? What words have all of the vowels in alphabetical order? Why do clocks use the Roman numeral IIII instead of IV for the number 4?

The important issues here are both patience and technique. Most of these puzzler questions circulate around and around, and experienced reference librarians become familiar with many of them. These are also the questions that get collected in the popular "fascinating facts" books like Cecil Adams's "The Straight Dope" series, David Feldman's "Imponderables," and many others. The same questions also turn up regularly on USENET newsgroups, and get collected in the FAQ files for the groups. They also recur on STUMPERS, the e-mail list where librarians post difficult reference questions.

## Problematic Questions

Some types of questions cause problems for some libraries, not because of their inherent difficulty, but for other reasons. The handling of these questions may be the subject of library policies, and they are often discussed and debated in meetings and on professional e-mail groups like LIBREF-L.

### CRISS-CROSS

Criss-cross directory questions have long been the bane of telephone reference. The questioner wants the librarian to look up a phone number and determine the name and address. Sometimes the patron also wants "nearbys"—the names and numbers of people who live in homes adjacent to the target person.

Many people call or visit the library looking for various types of directory information: names, addresses, and phone numbers in various combinations. The patron can be a stalker or a person seeking to identify someone who is harassing her, a person seeking a birth parent or a runaway child. The information from the directory may be used to benefit or harm another person. Most libraries view directories as published information, and place no limitations on the use of the information in the library.

Telephone reference presents a different set of issues, however. Many libraries get calls from collection agencies requesting several lookups. The calls can be time-consuming, and librarians are aware that most of these calls are not from local residents or businesses. Some of these callers are curt, unappreciative, or even rude, causing resentment from librarians.

Some libraries have had complaints from patrons—especially the "nearbys"—who have had information about them given out by the library. Although people could look up this information themselves in our libraries, having the librarian select the names of neighbors and give this information over the phone makes us more of an agent in the transaction.

These three concerns—time, service to nonlocal businesses, and patron privacy—have caused many libraries to institute special policies about criss-cross reference. Some limit the number of lookups that they will do over the phone. Some attempt to verify whether the call is coming from the local area. Many will do lookups of specific addresses or phone numbers, but won't do nearbys. Some libraries refuse to do any criss-cross reference over the phone, and some have simply stopped buying the directories.

The prevalence of these policies has apparently been noticed by the collection agencies. Paul Nelson, Director of the Middleton (WI) Public Library, writes:

> During the past ten years, I have noticed a change in approach from callers requesting criss-cross information. It used to be a very confidently spoken, "Crisscross, please!" Now it is a more hesitant, "Do you give out criss-cross information?"

Library policies and practices relating to criss-cross and

other kinds of directory information may need to be re-evaluated. The inexpensive, searchable availability of directory information on CD-ROM and on the World Wide Web means that we are probably getting fewer of these calls, and can expect them to continue to decline as collection agencies and other heavy users of this service acquire electronic access to this information. Easy, searchable access also means that libraries that have previously declined to answer these questions because they are time-consuming may find that they can now answer them quickly, especially if they have bookmarked one of the lookup services. At the very least, searchable access means that no library can solve the criss-cross problem by simply dropping the subscription to the directories, a "solution" mentioned by many participants in a criss-cross discussion on the e-mail group LIBREF-L.

## TRIVIA CONTESTS

Answering difficult questions is a job to us, but to many others, it's a game, a sport, a source of amusement. People watch television programs like *Jeopardy*, and play games like *Trivial Pursuit*, and many newspapers, magazines, and television and radio programs include regular trivia features.

Sometimes these features are contests, and our patrons turn to us for the answers. We may not be aware that some questions are for trivia contests, but often we are. The patron may tell us, or we may just guess that something more than coincidence is at play when we get eight phone calls in a row asking for the name of George Washington's horse.

Contest questions raise some issues for some librarians. They are deliberately difficult, sometimes deliberately tricky, and can be time-consuming. The same patron may have many questions to answer. And, for some librarians there is an ethical issue. Should the patron get credit (and possibly prizes) for work done by the librarian?

Usually, these contests are local, but two major corporations combined to send droves of people to libraries across the country when McDonald's sponsored a Disney trivia contest. This was the ultimate trivia nightmare. Many of the questions were very difficult, not things that could be quickly looked up in any reference book, since they were meant to be answered by viewing Disney videos. For example, one question asked what color trousers the Prince wore to the ball in *Cinderella*.

As librarians fielded the Disney trivia questions, something very interesting was happening on the Internet. Contest players began posting the Disney questions to various Disney-related newsgroups, where many were quickly answered, either by people who had already had the same contest question, or who simply knew the answer. Soon several people were assembling the questions and answers on Web pages, adding new ones as they were submitted. This was a good example of the Internet as a populist information utility, and shows the same process that happens over and over on the Net—questions are asked and answered on interest groups, and someone takes that information and organizes it as a Web page.

Librarians, meanwhile, dealt with the McDonald's questions as well as they could, although subsequent discussions on LIBREF-L and elsewhere showed a great deal of resentment over the contest. One person expressing a positive viewpoint, however, was Kelli Perkins of the Herrick Public Library in Holland, Michigan, who wrote:

> We are happy when anyone in the community thinks of the library as a resource. The woman who calls us with a McDonald's trivia question may be calling for the first time. Her question is not unimportant, rather it is a matter of time constraints, as it is with any question we receive at reference. All questions are treated equally and if not found in a reasonable amount of time, we explain that the patron should continue the search, we've done what we can. We are the busiest library in our cooperative of public libraries, but when members of the community reach out to us for information, we are going to be there.

The fact that some libraries consider contest questions to be a special problem, or a less-deserving category of reference, presents an interesting dilemma. If a patron simply states the question, without telling us the source of the question, he or she may get better service than if the reference librarian, through the reference interview process, elicits the information that the question is for a contest.

## PERSONAL INTERPRETATION AND RECOMMENDATIONS

Reference librarians are in the business of using a variety of resources to find information for our patrons. In the course of this work, we exercise our professional judgment in choosing and recommending information resources, but we do not interpret the information that we find. This is an especially important point in regard to medical, legal, and tax information, but the problem of interpretation can arise in any area.

For example, we often have people using reference resources to identify some object. These objects range from a postage stamp that they hope is valuable to an insect that they hope to exterminate. In these cases, librarians can work with the patron to find pictures and descriptions that seem to match the item, but it's up to the patron, not the librarian, to decide if their item is really the same, and if so, what to do about it.

Personal recommendations are also difficult issues for some reference librarians. The information that the patron shares in the course of the reference interview may suggest an answer to the librarian that is based on personal knowledge or opinion, not reference resources. Should the librarian ever offer the personal recommendation, labeled as such, or refrain?

Although professional literature indicates that personal recommendations are not appropriate, it seems that in practice librarians are divided on the issue. A new reference librarian posted a question on LIBREF-L describing an incident in which a patron had been looking for information on dental phobia, describing her bad experience with a dentist and her subsequent avoidance of the dentist. The librarian recommended her own dentist, but felt uncomfortable afterward with having done so, and sought advice from the members of the list. The response was about evenly divided between those who felt that recommending a dentist was inappropriate and those who felt that it was acceptable, especially if the librarians labeled it a personal recommendation.

## HOMEWORK QUESTIONS

Many libraries have formal or informal policies about providing help for homework questions, most stating that help will be provided but the student should perform the actual research. Where reference librarians really get into issues is when parents come to the library to collect material or perhaps perform research for their children. This topic comes up repeatedly on LIBREF-L and other e-mail lists, and always generates a lively discussion.

There seem to be two issues at play in these discussions. The first is a practical one: the difficulty of doing a reference interview with a third party, and not the person who is doing the project. The parents may not know the scope of the assignment, the focus or approach to the general topic, or restrictions on types of material that are to be used. A separate issue is the strong feelings that many librarians have that it is wrong for parents to take home material for their children, and that the students should be at the library selecting material for themselves.

In some cases, it sounds as if librarians conduct an aggressive reference interview with parents to make them realize that they do not have the answers for all of these questions, and to discourage parents from doing their children's work. Reference librarians should be careful not to allow our personal values into this or any other reference situation. We can help parents find general information on a topic that may be enough to start the research project, and suggest that the parent or student come back for more help as needed, without getting into the issue of why the student hasn't come to the library in the first place. The parent may have reasons, good or bad, for helping with the project, and we don't need to judge these reasons to provide whatever reasonable level of assistance we can.

## REFERENCE POLICY

The basic principles of reference are simple: we help patrons use the library's resources to find information or we find information for them; we provide them with information without interpretation; we provide help to all without imposing our own values or judgments. However, with the wide array of circumstances and questions that our patrons bring to the library, reference work is a complex enterprise.

A reference policy can be a helpful document in providing guidance to all staff members on dealing with the many problems and circumstances that are likely to arise. For example, the reference policy of the North Suburban Library System in Illinois (reprinted in Appendix A) provides guidance on general matters: priorities, statistics, referrals, follow-up, citing sources, and so forth. It also includes specific question guidelines, which include school assignments, contest questions, criss-cross and city directories, and other frequently troublesome question types.

Such a policy is helpful as a training tool and reference for staff members, but it is even more helpful as a guide in discussions of reference situations that arise. Reference staff members and library administrators both benefit from discussions of real and hypothetical circumstances and how the library's policy guidelines should be applied.

## INTAKE METHODS

### Walk-Up

How do people present their questions? In most libraries, most questions are asked in person—people approach the reference desk and ask their questions. There are certainly many advantages to this method. Many people do not enter the library with the intent of asking a reference question—they develop one after they arrive. A patron may arrive looking for some general information on a topic, which he or she finds in the circulating collection, but they may notice that some essential piece of information is missing—which becomes a reference question.

For example, a person may be preparing for a weekend visit by an old friend who has become a vegan: a strict vegetarian who eats no meat, dairy products, or eggs. She finds a few vegetarian cookbooks with some vegan recipes, which she'll check out, but notices that they don't include one thing she really wants—a vegan pancake recipe. This is now a reference question. Or a student may be looking for information on Guatemala for a report. He finds a few books and articles, which give him most of the information that he needs, but he notices that none of them show the Guatemalan flag, which is required. The student now approaches the reference desk to ask for a picture of the flag.

In fact, many patrons would prefer never to have to ask a reference question—they would rather walk into the library, easily locate a large and well-arranged collection of books on their topic of interest, containing all the answers to their questions. Most patrons prefer their information "to-go"—they would rather check out books and study the information in the comfort of home. In many instances, the need to ask a reference question is the result of the failure of the circulating collection to serve the needs of a particular patron, and represents a last resort. One person may have wanted a biography of Chester A. Arthur, but had to settle for photocopying a few pages from a reference book on the presidents; another may have wanted to take out a book on the clans of Scotland, but at the very least she needed a picture of the Royal Stewart tartan.

Reference librarians, handling these walk-up requests that come over from the circulating collection, are sometimes able to do more than just answer the specific inquiry that the patron brings to the desk; they may return with the patron to the circulating collection and help him or her find additional material to take home. All libraries should establish systems to ensure that those who have not found what they are looking for in the circulating collection will get some attention from the reference librarians. The most effective systems are simple: a circulation staff that asks, "Did you find what you were looking for?" and refers people to reference if they say they didn't, and reference librarians who leave the confines of the reference area periodically to check on patrons in the stacks and elsewhere, to offer assistance to patrons in need. The whole library staff, from the director to assistants shelving books, should be on the lookout for people who look like they might need help, and refer them to reference.

For most libraries, in-person assistance remains the primary means of handling reference questions—the patron approaches the reference desk and asks a question, or the reference librarian approaches the patron and offers assistance. The reference librarian may consult some ready-reference source and provide an answer to the question, or lead the patron to helpful sources of information, checking back later to make sure the patron is finding what he or she needs.

## Telephone Reference

Sometimes, however, a reference question is not related to some more general information search at the library. For whatever reason, a person has a need for some specific piece of information. A man is planning an anniversary party for his parents and needs to know what songs were popular in a certain year. He doesn't want information on the musical trends of the times or any other information— he just needs the names of a couple of songs to give the band. The woman with the vegan guest may only be planning to cook breakfast, and may only need that pancake recipe, not a whole cookbook. Someone needs a quote from Shakespeare identified for a speech, the date of the attack on Pearl Harbor verified for a newsletter article, the address of the Sierra Club, or the number of calories in a Big Mac.

When a patron doesn't need to be in the library, and just wants some piece of information, he or she may pick up the phone and call the library. Telephone reference can be convenient, saving the patron a trip. However, there are logistical problems for librarians trying to provide fair service to patrons both in the library and on the phone. What happens when you are working with a patron and the phone rings? Do you put the person in front of you "on hold" while you answer the phone? If so, do you then put the person on the phone on hold until you finish with the

first patron? If so, do you then take the phone call, while
another patron in person stands there waiting for your attention?

Trying to balance the needs of phone patrons with the
needs of those in the building is a troublesome issue, and
one that raises questions of fairness on all sides. For example, in a posting on PUBLIB, Karen Stipek of the
Alachua County Library District writes about the practice
of interrupting walk-in patrons to answer the phone, and
notes that this is a practice that makes her "crazy" when
she's on the other side of the service desk in a library or
store. It's frustrating to be in the middle of asking a question or making a purchase and have someone else "jump
the queue" and get served first by making a phone call.

> . . . the practice of interrupting walk-in patrons to an-
> swer the phone. When I am on the other side of any
> service desk, whether in a store or a library, that
> makes me crazy. There I am, in mid-question or mid-
> purchase, and somebody else gets to jump the queue
> by virtue of making a phone ring.

Ideally, this problem is solved by having a separate telephone reference service line that is not answered by librarians who are covering the reference desk, but trying to staff
two separate reference stations can be difficult, especially
since it's difficult to predict the balance between phone and
in-person questions for any given shift. Some libraries don't
staff a separate desk, but divert reference calls to another
location during peak hours. In other libraries, in-house and
telephone reference patrons are given equal priority and
taken in order, with the phone patrons placed on hold until
it's their turn for service. Many libraries have a voice-mail

system that takes messages when the reference librarians are engaged with patrons, with calls returned as time permits.

## Offline Methods

Libraries have tended to do almost all reference in a manner that computer people would call *online*, and telecommunications people would call *synchronous*. Whether in person or on the phone, the reference librarian and the person with the question need to be directly connected while the question is communicated and the answer is located. There are advantages to this mode of business, of course. If the question is not just important, but urgent—an answer is needed right this minute—the immediacy of a face-to-face or voice-to-voice communication is needed. If the question is complex, a conversation (in person or by phone) may be needed. But for errand questions, where the patron can easily articulate the question and the reference librarian can easily locate an answer, an *offline, asynchronous* method might be more beneficial.

Offline modes can be high tech, like reference service by e-mail, or low tech, like reference service by postal mail. The advantages to patrons are that they get to, in essence, drop off their question, and get back their answer without having to wait in person or on the phone line while the librarian looks up the answer. Offline reference is of special benefit to patrons who are exceptionally busy, or whose hours or schedule aren't a good match for the library's, or who simply prefer the impersonal approach.

The advantage to the library is that instead of taking every question in person or on the phone and trying to answer them all immediately, questions submitted offline by mail, e-mail, fax, or telephone answering machine, can be distributed and answered by the reference staff as time permits. Even for questions that are a little more complex than ready reference, the quality of the reference work is often improved by working offline, because of a lack of distraction, and the ability to route questions to the most appropriate staff members.

## QUESTION-AND-ANSWER SERVICES

When considering offering reference service by e-mail and other offline methods of submitting questions to the library, reference librarians often worry about the lack of a reference interview. However, many patrons find it much simpler to organize and express their questions in writing than in person.

We can see this tendency in a traditional alternative to library reference—the many question-and-answer or "Ask-the-Expert" columns that appear in newspapers and magazines. Some columns are general, like "Dear Abby," "Ann Landers," and "The Straight Dope," while others are limited to such topics as chess, science, health, beauty, home repair, or investments. In writing, people seem generally to be able to organize their question and provide enough background information to allow for a good answer.

An interesting reference training experiment is to gather a group of these questions from the newspaper, and have a pair of librarians role-play these as reference questions. The nature of spoken communication is such that it is difficult for the questioner to rattle off four or five sentences without a break, and the reference interview is necessary just to accommodate the rhythm of conversation.

Of course, it must be noted that columnists have one

great advantage over librarians—they get to pick and choose among the questions submitted, and presumably reject those that are confusing, incomprehensible, or simply too difficult to answer!

### Ask the Expert

In addition to Ask an Expert columns in print publications, there are also columns on various Web sites. Some, in fact, are associated with print columns. The popular "Car Talk" column by Click and Clack (otherwise known as Tom and Ray Magliozzi), featured in over 200 newspapers, is archived on the Car Talk Web site (*cartalk.cars.com/Columns/*). The large collection of questions and answers can be browsed by date or searched by keyword.

One interesting column is by Jack Larkin, Director of Research, Collections and Library at Old Sturbridge Village, a living history museum in Sturbridge, Massachusetts. Larkin's "Ask Jack" column is a regular feature of the *Old Sturbridge Village Kids* newsletter, answering all kinds of questions about life in the 1830s. There is now an Ask Jack page on the Old Sturbridge Village Web site, (*www.osv. org/pages/askjack.htm*). The Ask Jack answers are warm and friendly, and, as in the case of his answer to the question "Did kids in the 1830s make snowmen like we do?" Larkin not only answers the question, but tells just how he tracked down this information.

Ask-an-Expert features of various types are found on many Web sites, on subjects as diverse as fly fishing and Amish life. They are particularly popular as part of health and parenting sites. These sites generally accumulate archives, which may be browsed by subject or searched by keyword.

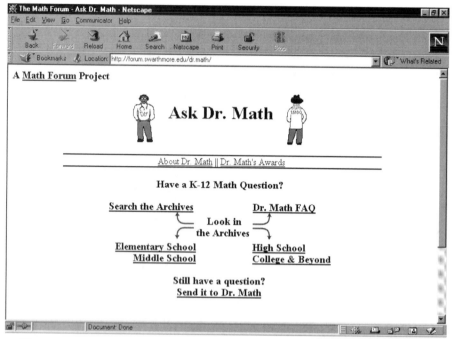

**Figure 6–1. Ask Dr. Math.**

One particularly successful Ask-an-Expert site is Ask Dr. Math, (*forum.swarthmore.edu/dr.math/*), a service from Swarthmore College's Math Forum. "Dr. Math" (Figure 6–1) is actually a large group of volunteer math students who answer questions submitted by students, kindergarten through high school. There is a FAQ file, plus searchable archives divided into elementary, middle and high school levels.

Many questions appear here that are also frequent library reference questions, including "Why was the letter *m* selected to represent slope?" (As is the case of many perennial reference questions, there are a few possibilities but no definitive answer to this one.) The Dr. Math students

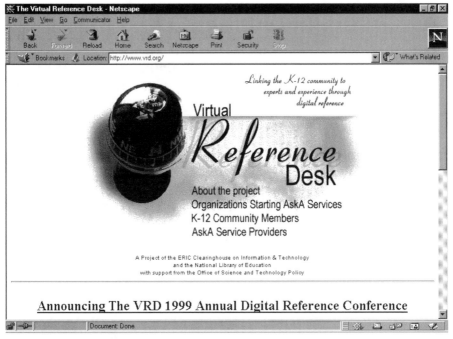

**Figure 6–2. The Virtual Reference Desk.**

do an excellent job of offering simple, understandable explanations, often with many real-life examples. For example, the answer to the question "Why does a negative number times a negative number equal a positive?" includes two mathematical proofs, but also some real-world examples, involving paying bills, walking on a number line, and driving a car.

### Virtual Reference Desk

The Virtual Reference Desk (*www.vrd.org*) is working to build the foundations for a national cooperative digital reference service by providing training, support, and re-

sources to offer Ask-an-Expert digital reference services on
the World Wide Web (Figure 6–2). The Virtual Reference
Desk (*www.vrd. org*) is a project of the ERIC Clearing-
house on Information and Technology and the National
Library of Education, and its focus is on services to students from kindergarten through high school.

R. David Lankes of ERIC explains the importance of
digital reference services in a world where students are offered an incredible array of electronic information resources. "Static Web pages and impersonal software
cannot match the power of person-to-person communication in meeting the needs of the K-12 community" (Lankes,
1999). The Virtual Reference Desk (VRD) fosters the personal interaction between subject experts and students
through a variety of activities, including developing guidelines and training material for the provision of high-quality reference service by the Ask-an-Expert services. This
interaction is important since many of these services are
provided by subject experts who may not have experience in
the reference process, or experience working with children.

The VRD's document Information Mentoring: Guidelines for Providing Reference Service to K-12 (*www.vrd.
org/training/training.html*) gives many examples of the reference interview in the electronic environment, and the elements of a complete answer. The guidelines stress the need
to teach the information-seeking process showing the path
to the answer, including search engines and search terms
that were used, and to explain why certain resources were
selected. They also note that:

> . . . it is a good idea to refer students to their school
> library media specialists (LMS) in order to stress that
> their LMS are information experts in their schools and

can guide them to local and remote resources. Students and educators should be aware that digital reference services can supplement—and not replace—the information resources and services available in school media centers and other libraries (Lankes, 1998).

An Ask-an-Expert services developed primarily outside of the realm of librarianship. Many services are sponsored by colleges and universities, museums, associations, and individuals with a wealth of subject knowledge and an interest in sharing it. The VRD's guidelines help participating services understand such professional issues as the need to provide authoritative, unbiased answers to questions, the need for training and review of those answering questions, and the need to maintain the privacy of users of the service.

The Virtual Reference Desk plans to develop resources that will link the Ask-an-Expert services into a true, distributed digital reference service. They currently maintain AskA+ Locator, a subject guide to existing services, and they hope to develop an "incubator" to develop new services in subject areas not yet covered, and a program to match questions with appropriate services. Perhaps the most exciting possibility for reference librarians is the creation of a knowledge base of questions and answers from all the participating services, which should become a unusual and valuable collective reference work.

### Ask Jeeves

Ask Jeeves is a World Wide Web site (*www.askjeeves. com*) that uses a combination of sophisticated software and subject expertise to provide connections to authoritative answers to common questions.

Ask Jeeves has a large database of individual questions and question templates. The individual questions are things like, "Why is the sky blue?" and "What is the population of the world?" and "How are new USENET newsgroups created and maintained?" Most of the questions, however, are in the form of question templates. For example, there are question templates for "Where can I find information about the movie [blank]?" and "Where can I find information on the American history topic [blank]?" and "What is the diameter of [blank]?" Each question template has a list that can be used to fill in the blanks, and some questions have more than one list of variables.

You ask Jeeves a question in natural language—for example, "How do you tie a necktie?" Jeeves runs through the database of questions, looking for ones that might be relevant. In this case, Jeeves will respond with the one matching question, "How can I learn to tie a necktie?" The question "What's the national anthem of Italy?" matches the question "Where can I hear or find the lyrics for the national anthem of Italy?" Some questions will give you several possible matches. You select the best match and click on the Ask button to retrieve the Web page that has been selected as the answer to this question. In the case of the necktie question, for example, you would get a necktie tutorial from Learn2.com (*www.learn2.com*), many of whose excellent tutorials have been selected as answers in Ask Jeeves. In the case of the national anthem, we are connected to a page with the words, music, and sound files for the Italian national anthem, from an authoritative source—the Italian embassy.

This combination of artificial intelligence (used by the software to match the natural language questions to the questions in the database) and human intelligence and judgment (used by the researchers and subject specialists at Ask Jeeves) makes this a powerful way of finding specific information on the World Wide Web. The software does more than just match keywords, and knows, for example, that a question containing the word *moon* should be related to the *Apollo 11 lunar landing*. It also responds to the question "Who was the twentieth President of the United States?" with the question template "Where can I find information about U.S. President [James A. Garfield]?" and to the question "What is the largest planet?" with question templates "What is the diameter of [Jupiter]?" and "Where can I find statistical information about the celestial body [Jupiter]?"

For some questions, it knows that it needs more information, and asks for it. For example, if you ask Jeeves the question "Who is my U.S. Representative" you will get two question templates: "Who are the U.S. Senators and House Members representing [Alabama]?" (with an options list of all the state names) and "Who is the Representative for the zip code [blank]?" and you, of course, need to enter your own zip code.

Of course, Ask Jeeves is not perfect and working with it is not like asking questions of a real human being. It has difficulty with certain simple questions, especially if there aren't any near matches in its database of questions, or if there are two different concept words. For example, a question on the number of people executed as witches in Salem caused Jeeves to present the question template "Where can I find the [population] for the city [Salem,

Mass.]? (also Salem, Ark.; Salem, Ill.; etc.) as well as "Where can I learn about the Halloween creature [witches]?" and "Where can I learn about the religious belief [Wicca]?"

This intermediate step of presenting you with possible questions and allowing you to select among them is Jeeves's version of a reference interview, a chance to make sure that the person with the question and the provider of answers understand each other. The question, "Where can I find information about sharks?" will get two questions in response: "Where can I find the current [team report & general info] for the NHL team [San Jose Sharks]?" and "Where can I find information on the animal [sharks]?"

As a supplement to its database of questions, Ask Jeeves submits keywords from your question to Lycos, Excite, InfoSeek, and other Internet search engines, and presents those results along with its selection of questions thus, even if our question doesn't match anything in the Jeeves database, Jeeves may still be able to point you in the right direction. Ask Jeeves is currently providing a version of its answer service through AltaVista, is licensing its technology for intranets, and has developed a children's version, Ask Jeeves for Kids (*www.ajkids.com*).

## LIBRARY REFERENCE QUESTIONS ON THE WORLD WIDE WEB

Many libraries of all types and sizes present files of reference questions and answers on their World Wide Web sites. These files make interesting reading, and also serve as an excellent public relations tool to show the public the kind of service that libraries can provide.

### Falmouth Public Library

The Falmouth (Mass.) Public Library has a Reference Desk FAQ as part of its World Wide Web site (*www.capecod. net/fpl/faq.html*). This is a list of telephone reference questions recently handled by the Falmouth staff, with answers, and an archive of older questions.

The questions include definitions of terms (such as *arachibutyrophobia*, the fear that peanut butter will stick to the roof of the mouth); addresses (for example, the address of former Massachusetts Governor Elliot Richardson); quotations (such as the Helen Keller quote about life being an adventure); and local information (including information on a stamp collecting club). There is a fascinating array of general factual questions, including the amount of sugar in a medium orange, Tom Thumb's real name, and the inventor of cotton candy. There are also many bibliographic identification questions, including half-remembered titles (a book about religion with the words *cross* and *mushroom* in the title.)

This is not a database of searchable questions, and most are so specific that they can hardly be "frequently asked" questions, so this is not a particularly useful resource in terms of finding answers. The files of questions and answers make interesting reading, however, and do add interesting content to the library Web site. The most important purpose of these lists, however, is that they show the public what kind of reference questions come to the public library, and the kind of answers that they can expect. Many of the responses here go beyond a simple factual answer, and include information on the home access to the online catalog of CLAMS (the library consortium of which Falmouth is a member), Interlibrary Loan, having articles faxed from other libraries, and sources that can be used in the library, as well as an invitation to come to the library for more help.

### Chicago Public Library

The Chicago Public Library takes a similar approach to Falmouth on its Web site, but archives of questions are divided by month—for example, "Frequently Asked Reference Questions—October" (*www.chipublib.org/008subject/005genref/gisquestion.html*). Some questions in each monthly file relate to the events or concerns of the month, and others don't. For example, the October file includes the end of Daylight Savings Time and the celebration of Sweetest Day, as well as such general questions as the motto of the United States Postal Service and the most popular dog breeds in the United States. The individual monthly files are not searchable at this time. There is a special file for Halloween questions, which is a handy feature. All answers include a citation to the source, almost always a standard reference book. A few answers include links to Web sites.

As with Falmouth's collection of reference questions and answers, Chicago's collection serves not so much as an archive for others with the same question as a browsing collection of fascinating facts, and a public relations tool, demonstrating the kind of service that reference librarians perform.

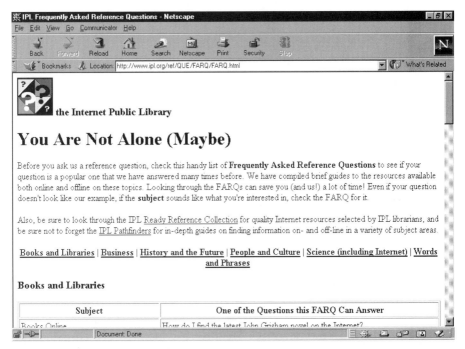

**Figure 6–3. The Internet Public Library's FAQ Collection.**

### *Internet Public Library*

The Internet Public Library (Figure 6–3) answers reference questions, and has put together a collection of FAQ files called You Are Not Alone (Maybe) (*www.ipl.org/ref/QUE/FARQ/FARQ.html*). Although their list includes a few specific questions, including the origin of the phrases *once in a blue moon* and *publish or perish*, most are question categories. For example, there are listings for Anniversary Gifts, Automobile Blue Books, Company Profiles, and Citing Electronic Information. Each of these categories leads to a file that provides an answer with a citation, and/or pointers to more information. In some cases, such as the one on Finding Magazine and Journal Articles, the Internet Public Library staff explains the limits of their service and of Internet searching, and refers people to their local library for more help.

## FOUR STRATEGIES FOR SUCCESS

Reference librarians offer a variety of services, and interact with people in a number of ways. However, it's the activity of answering questions that occupies a major part of our time, and that defines us in the minds of many people.

1. Be prepared to handle all types of questions.
   Some of us are better at certain types of questions than others. Work with other reference staff members to improve your technique on all types of questions. Train all staff members to be aware of how often one type of question can masquerade as another, and to use the reference interview to make sure the question is understood before beginning the search for an answer.

2. Have a reference policy to handle problematic situations.
   How does your library handle criss-cross questions, content questions, and other kinds of problematic questions? To ensure that all staff members handle these situations in the same way, the library needs a reference policy that covers the issues. All members of the reference staff should be familiar with the pro-

visions of the policy, and it should be consulted, discussed, and reviewed on a regular basis. A sample policy appears in Appendix A.

3. Attend to the question itself, and not the circumstances.
   Reference librarians are very good at handling all types of questions in a nonjudgmental manner, and not allowing our personal, philosophical, religious, and political opinions affect our response. However, sometimes we find it harder to be objective about the circumstances of the question: a parent doing homework for a child, a person phoning instead of coming to the library, a student who prefers electronic resources even when print sources would serve his need better. We need to make sure that our personal feelings don't affect the level of attention that we give to all questions.

4. Use those questions and answers for public relations purposes!
   Many people are only dimly aware of reference services, and have no idea what kinds of questions we can answer. Don't tell people about your service, show them by example what you do. Write about interesting reference questions and their answers for your library newsletter or the local newspaper, post them on a bulletin board, or use them as interesting content on your library's Web site. They make great reading, and are wonderful advertising for your library's reference service.

# Chapter 7

# Reference Librarians as Trainers and Pathfinders

Libraries today have access to an amazing array of all kinds of information, in many different formats and languages, with greatly varying depth, quality, points of view, accuracy, and authority. It's an exciting but confusing new world. To make sense of it all, we need training for ourselves, and in turn we need to provide training, support, and guidance to our library users.

## TRAINING

There was a time when reference librarians received their training in graduate school and on their first job and could comfortably maintain and develop their skills through experience, the review of new material, reading professional journals, and participating in professional associations. Now, however, we are faced with an environment where, in addition to these traditional types of professional development, we need frequent training in order to use the array of electronic systems and services that have come to our libraries.

With print-based resources, reference librarians had to understand the intellectual content of the material, but there were no commands or keystrokes to learn. Now, every new electronic resource requires us to learn procedures and protocols, with new versions or new options coming out quickly. In addition to the electronic resources themselves, we need training to use and manage the computers that we're using for access. Working with the Web-based version of a reference database and printing, saving, e-mailing, and downloading files may involve understanding a combination of commands and menus involving the operating system, the browser, and of the specific product itself. Resolving a printing problem may involve working with any or all of the above, plus security software, network setup, hardware, and cabling.

In addition to meeting our own training needs, reference librarians are increasingly involved in providing training to patrons. This training may involve scheduled presentations or workshops, individual assistance at the workstations, ongoing support by phone or e-mail, and the preparation of various kinds of training material.

We have come to the point where almost all library staff members are involved in some aspect of training. Reference librarians receive training for themselves and provide training to other staff members and to library users, while library administrators struggle to provide enough resources for the increasing burden of training. Staff training is expensive, not only in terms of fees for workshops and sometimes travel expenses, but in time away from service and the staffing arrangements necessary for coverage. Training for library users is also expensive, in the amount of staff time needed for both preparation and presentation.

## BIBLIOGRAPHIC INSTRUCTION

Bibliographic instruction is the term generally used in academic libraries for a formal program of instruction in library skills. Bibliographic instruction, or BI, has many forms, including library tours as part of freshman orientation, credit or noncredit courses on library skills, and single-session workshops on the use of different library resources. Often librarians will work with the faculty to offer bibliographic instruction for a class, often in preparation for a major project or research paper.

Until recently, bibliographic instruction was generally only practiced by school and college librarians. Public libraries sometimes gave library tours, often as part of a class visit, and librarians would visit schools and local organizations to talk about the library and its services, but library instruction was only offered on an individual basis, as part of helping users with a particular problem. With the arrival of the online catalog and CD-ROM and online periodicals products, library users began to demand something more. Some library users wanted more instruction in these systems because they found them too difficult to use on their own, while others were intrigued by the possibilities of advanced techniques and wanted to know more.

Coping with these new resources and especially with the World Wide Web, many public libraries have been overwhelmed with the amount of support that so many library users at public workstations need, and have started offering workshops and training sessions for patrons as a way to help a whole group of people learn the basics and become more independent users. These workshops may be lecture/demonstration sessions, hands-on training, or a combination of the two. Most libraries begin by offering introductory workshops on their online catalog, other electronic databases, and the Internet. Workshops on particular subject interests, especially job-hunting, genealogy, investments, health, and travel information, are also popular. Many libraries have had great success with special classes for different age groups, including children, teenagers, and senior citizens.

One of the oldest and most basic debates in librarianship is whether we should focus on service or on education. Should we just find people the information that they want, or should we teach them how to find it themselves? But this is really a false dichotomy. Librarians should focus on service, with the understanding that sometimes education is an important element of service. Many public libraries are responding to a new demand for training, and many academic librarians are finding their BI services in more demand now than ever before.

There's another reason for all types of libraries to move from offering individual instruction to more formal training opportunities: remote access. Now that many users of public, academic, and special libraries have home or office access to the electronic resources provided by the library, they are interested in receiving some training to find what they need when they are on their own.

## THE ART OF TRAINING

Many reference librarians now find that training is an essential and increasingly important part of their jobs. Ironically, most librarians have received no formal training to be trainers. Training has become a recognized profession in its own right, with a substantial body of research and professional literature that should interest librarians who find themselves gradually becoming professional trainers.

Training is different from education in the sense that training focuses on the transmission of a set of skills rather than a body of knowledge. Training may be an element of a continuing education or professional development program for staff, or a bibliographic instruction program for library users.

Training generally seeks to answer the question "How do I do this?" In terms of electronic reference resources, training instructs the user in how to perform different types of searches, evaluate the results, and view, print, or otherwise use the text, graphics, sound files, and so on, that were retrieved. But in order to be successful, training almost always includes elements beyond just how-to instructions; the learner must understand not only how a certain resource can be used, but when and why it's appropriate to use.

### Learning Styles

Much has been written over the past decade on the concept of learning styles—the different ways that individuals learn. Although we all learn in a variety of ways, most people tend to fall into one of three primary learning styles: auditory, visual, and kinesthetic.

Auditory learners learn through hearing, and they like lectures, speeches, traditional classroom presentations, and detailed explanations. This is the learning style to which the school system is traditionally geared.

Visual learners need to see something to learn it. Visual learners like pictures, charts, graphs, diagrams, and other types of visual aids. Visual learners were disadvantaged in traditional classrooms and with print-based reference material, but are generally thriving in the highly visual environment of the World Wide Web.

Kinesthetic learners learn by doing. They like hands-on training, and are not afraid to pick up the mouse and jump right in—in fact, they often forget to listen for instruction since they prefer to try things themselves. They prefer on-the-job training (or, better yet, the opportunity to explore a resource themselves) to any type of formal training.

Although, we all learn through a combination of auditory, visual, and kinesthetic means, in most people one of these three learning styles predominates. Ideally, each staff member and each library user would receive training customized to his or her personal learning style, but this approach is clearly not practical. Two things can be done, however, to help all learners get the information they need.

The first is to provide a variety of training opportunities, so that learners can choose ones that suit their own style. In some organizations, all staff members are expected to attend a certain number of formal training sessions and collect certificates, which are recorded as part of the performance review process. This works well for some staff members, but not for those who learn better on their own.

In some colleges, the same basic bibliographic instruction is provided to all incoming freshman, as a part of orientation. These rigid systems are examples of what professional trainers disdainfully refer to as "sheep-dipping." Everyone attends identical sessions as a rite of passage, and it's the attendance, not learning the material, that matters.

Sometimes accommodating the needs of those with alternative learning styles is as simple as providing a collection of books, videos, and interactive media for staff use, and making sure that those who prefer to learn independently be given time and equipment to do so. For library users, printed and Web-based guides, help screens, and other written material help the independent learners develop their skills.

The other way to accommodate the different learning styles is to make sure that all training sessions include a mixture of auditory, visual, and kinesthetic elements. Adding some well-planned visual aids (which can include projected material or such low-tech visual tools as flip charts and the blackboard) will help keep the attention of the visual learners. For the kinesthetic learners, any opportunity for hands-on experience will help. Kinesthetic learners also benefit from any chance to get out of their seats, including breaks and break-out sessions. You can satisfy both the visual and the kinesthetic learners by having volunteers record important points on large sheets of paper and hang them around the room—the visual learners find the evolving display helps focus their attention and the kinesthetic learners love to be up there fooling around with the markers and the tape.

The same principle of including material for different learning styles should also be applied to handouts and training material designed for reference and independent learning. Librarians often like to document things, and they produce manuals with page after page of well-crafted prose. There's nothing wrong with this material, but it must be supplemented with other approaches: screen prints and diagrams for the visual learners, and exercises for the kinesthetic learners. Look at some of the popular computer books in your collection for ideas. One of the reasons for the success of the "Dummies" books and other popular series is that they supplement the paragraphs of prose with pictures, diagrams and boxed tips, tricks, and warnings.

### Ambience

Ambience is important to all learners. People are able to learn more if they are comfortable and free from distractions. Many libraries are adding electronic classrooms or other training space to their facilities. College libraries without their own training space may reserve classrooms for library sessions. Public libraries sometimes schedule training sessions during hours when the library is closed, in order to have dedicated access to a group of public workstations. Training space should be designed to have good lighting, sound and temperature control, adequate space, and comfortable chairs.

Independent learners also need appropriate space and facilities. This can be as simple as providing staff members with access to a workstation in an office or workroom, away from the reference desk. Giving staff members time and space for independent learning, exploration, and practice is one of the most beneficial things that a library can do for staff development.

In some circumstances, serving refreshments is appropriate. Refreshments help reduce the tension that many people feel about training situations, and tend to promote social interaction among the attendees. The refreshments for training sessions don't need to be fancy, but it's worth a little effort to lay things out nicely. This appeals to the visual people, and conveys a message of respect toward the users. It's a way of saying, "we consider this to be an important occasion." (So take the doughnuts out of the box!)

### Beyond Learning Styles

Beyond the three basic learning styles, many other differences among groups of people can affect their behavior in training situations. There are basic differences in brain dominance, for example, with creative right-brain thinkers preferring a different type of training from analytical left-brain thinkers. Some psychologists believe that there is a basic difference in motivational orientation—some people have a primarily positive motivation, looking for new skills and resources, while others have a primarily negative motivation, looking for ways to avoid trouble. We can also divide people in terms of their relationship to technology—some people are early adapters, and want to try anything new, while others are more reluctant, and don't want to try anything until it's well established.

There are also basic differences based on generation. Older people, raised during the golden age of radio, tend to be auditory learners; Baby Boomers, raised on television, are more visual; and younger people, raised on computers and video games, thrive in situations that are interactive and participatory.

In addition to age, there are also career-related issues that are especially troubling among librarians in training situations. There are some major differences among three groups: early-career, mid-career, and late-career professionals. These differences are not just related to age, but to the major changes that have happened in our profession.

Early-career professionals, those who entered the profession in the past ten years, knew what they were getting into, and generally have a positive approach toward computers and the training demands of fast-evolving technology. This openness is true whether someone chose librarianship at the age of 21 or as a midlife career change. Late-career people, those within ten years of retirement, sometimes have emotional issues, when, instead of being honored for their knowledge and experience, they find themselves struggling to keep up with technology in a profession that has changed almost beyond recognition. Mid-career professionals are all over the place—some find the challenges of new technology exciting, while others are finding the new increasing pace of change stressful, and are not looking forward to another 25 years in a profession that they perhaps wouldn't choose today.

In staff training, these emotional and attitudinal issues may be as important and as difficult to deal with as differences in learning style. In training library users, especially college students, we find some of these same issues. Those who have recently returned to college may be overwhelmed by the changes in technology, and be dismayed to discover that their old library skills, based on print encyclopedias and the *Readers' Guide*, are now obsolete. Younger students who are uncomfortable with computers may be feeling even more stress, as they realize how pervasive technology has become and how important computer skills will be when they enter the workforce.

## TRAINING TECHNIQUES

The most effective training for all learners, perhaps especially those with anxiety or attitude problems, always builds from existing strengths, and works from familiar material to unfamiliar material. Learning can only take place when interest is aroused. Richard Saul Wurman writes, "Learning can be defined as the process of remembering what you are interested in" (Wurman, 1980, p. 138). Always approach the training from the point of view of your learners. What will be interesting and useful for them to know? How can you respond to their (usually) unspoken question: "Why should I care about this?"

### Keep It Real

Always connect new material to familiar experiences, comparing new systems with known ones, including print ones. For example, to teach Boolean operators, don't use abstract examples, like **A AND (B OR C)**, or contrived examples like **CAT AND DOG NOT MOUSE**. What could the patron possibly have asked for that would cause you to construct that particular search? Almost as bad as the use of **A AND (B OR C)** is the sole reliance on Venn diagrams to explain Boolean logic. Some people, especially visual learners, understand Venn diagrams, but other types of learners find them hopelessly confusing. Incorporating a variety of instructional techniques that address a variety of learners' styles works best.

It's important to teach searching techniques using real-life examples. Instead of **A AND (B OR C)** use an example like **ART AND (JAPAN OR JAPANESE)**. Better yet, use several different examples, explaining the thought process involved in the selection and arrangement of search terms. Using recent reference questions, new books, and current events as the source of search examples can help keep your training both real and relevant.

And speaking of "Boolean operators," avoid using unnecessary jargon, and always define all new or possibly unfamiliar terms when you must use them. For terms that you think are new to many people in the group, write the term on the board, call attention to it on the handout, or otherwise make sure that people can see it as well as hear it. For a term that is probably familiar, you should still make sure that you give the definition when you first use the term. For written material, you can supply a glossary as well as trying to define all terms within the text. On Web pages, you can make terms hyperlinks to a definition or explanation.

In presentations and training sessions, you need to watch people to see if anyone looks confused by terms that you use. Never assume that people understand everything just because they aren't raising their hands and asking questions. Most people fear being the only one who doesn't understand something, and they would prefer to hide that fact. When someone does interrupt with a question, thank that person for reminding you to define the term, and make him or her feel comfortable about having asked.

## The Successful Trainer: Some Points to Consider

### Respect

Teaching takes place in the context of a relationship. This is true whether you are training people that you work with every day or working with a group of people that you have never met. If you expect people to give you their attention, you need to come to them with respect.

If you don't respect the people you are supposed to teach, examine your own feelings to see what's really going on. If the learners strike you as obstinate, unrealistic, crazy, lazy, or the like, find out more about them. Are personal or job issues interfering with the training process? You may need to work around such issues, but it helps to be aware of them.

### Preparation

There are no shortcuts on this one. You need to know the material thoroughly, and know how to break it down into the essential elements. You need to work out what you want to say and how you want to say it, work out how to incorporate visual and kinesthetic elements into a presentation, and decide what kinds of handouts and other supporting material you need. You need to work with others in your organization to make sure that you understand the goals of the training and the needs of the learner.

Once you have done all of this preparation and come up with a perfect program, the tendency is to present it the same way, over and over. However, to maintain and even improve the quality of the program, it's important to repeat the preparation process for each presentation and make sure that you make changes to incorporate new material based on changed circumstances and feedback from learners. Even if the basic material remains the same, it's a good idea to vary the examples you use, just to keep the material fresh and interesting for yourself as well as the learners.

### Humor

You don't need to stand up and tell jokes, but it's hard to train people effectively without a little humor to keep their attention.

*Continued on following page*

Humor is the reward for listening. Laughter also helps people relax and feel accepted, and reduces the anxiety that many people feel in a training situation.

**Positive Reinforcement**

Human beings, like other animals, learn primarily through positive reinforcement. With adults, the rewards are usually subtle and internal: professional pride, the opportunity for advancement, the respect of peers. If the training is practical and is based on an understanding of the real needs of the learners, the positive reinforcement will come naturally as people learn skills that will help them on the job or in their academic or personal pursuits.

The strongest motivators are these natural and intrinsic ones. Most people find any type of personal recognition a very strong motivator. However, in certain situations you can introduce additional rewards, including awards, certificates, and even small gifts or prizes. Chocolate is well known for its motivational power, which is one of the reasons that it is available in so many shapes (including computers and diskettes). It's best to use these special treats for major training events, such as a major systems migration.

However, you should be careful about the use of external rewards for training, since for many people they trivialize and cheapen the training experience. Assume that your learners want to improve their knowledge and skills. If you can help them do that, they will feel rewarded for their time and effort.

**Patience**

However carefully you have prepared and however much you know about training, it still can be a frustrating experience. This is probably more true for inside trainers than for outside trainers, who are not around after the training to see how much or how little of the material covered may be retained and applied.

Keep learning from the training that you do, and pay careful attention to the support system that people need after training: handouts, access to workstations, time to practice, and follow-up sessions, for example.

### Avoid Demo-itis

Most of us have seen many sales presentations of different computer systems over the years, and have been the victims of demo-itis. Vendor representatives want to show off their system, and come up with one or two perfect examples for each feature. They make sure each example works perfectly and doesn't run into any complicated screens or authority control issues or other complications. The system performs beautifully at the demo, but the real-life experience is far less satisfying.

The vendors can hardly be blamed for presenting their systems in the best possible light, but library trainers should resist the urge to show only examples that work perfectly. It's better to show one or two simple examples, to convey the principle, and then some others that show common problems. On the other hand, it's important to avoid the other pitfall—showing obscure situations that rarely occur to a group of beginners.

### Handouts, Follow-up, and Evaluation

Many people attending training sessions worry about missing or forgetting important information, and they attempt to take copious notes. The tension of trying to make sure they don't miss anything has a negative effect on their ability to learn, and the note taking can be a distraction. To relieve this tension and reduce the need for notes, you can provide handouts so users know that they will have something to refer to afterward. Some trainers prefer not to distribute the handout until after the session, to help people focus on the trainer rather than having them read the handout during the session. In this case, they inform their audiences that the handouts will be distributed later so they don't have to resort to note taking.

Many trainers now create Web pages for training sessions, which can be used for projection by the trainer and for hands-on work by the students. Using these pages can eliminate the need for paper handouts, as long as the students know exactly how to connect to the training page after the session.

Whether you are working with library staff or with patrons, it's helpful to provide some means of follow-up. This can be as simple as putting your e-mail address on handouts or the session page, and telling people that you are available to answer questions. When you are working with patrons, make sure they know where, when, and how to get help from a reference librarian. Every bibliographic instruction session has two purposes—to teach students about some group of reference resources, and to acquaint them with the existence of intelligent, well-educated, highly skilled, helpful human beings called reference librarians.

Many trainers collect evaluation forms at the end of a training session. The problem with this practice is that attendees don't know yet whether the training was successful; they don't know how much information they will retain, and how useful it will be to them when they try to apply it themselves. Try to find a way to gather evaluations from people a week or two after the session, when they will have a better idea of what they really learned.

### Flow

It's a good idea to provide training opportunities in various doses. A full-day, formal training session is like a flood of information poured over the heads of the learners. This can be an effective way of presenting a lot of information, although there is the risk of overwhelming the learner. A 15-minute session in which one staff member demonstrates some new feature or function to a few colleagues might instead be seen as a few gulps.

Some of the most useful training, however, could be called drip-drip-drip training. Individual bits of information are disseminated in some manner. These bits of information can be demonstrations of new Web sites that are particularly useful, search tips for the online catalog or reference databases, or other individual nuggets of knowledge. They can be distributed in various ways—in newsletters or newspaper columns, or through e-mail.

## PATHFINDERS

One important function of reference librarians is to serve as guides to information resources in different areas. We do this for patrons on an individual basis all the time. When a student tells us he's working on a term paper on gun control, we make sure he knows how to find books in the online catalog, articles in a periodicals database, World Wide Web resources, and other specialized resources. In effect, we are creating a pathfinder on the fly for the each patron who comes to the library with a general inquiry.

In every library, however, there are certain predictable information needs. These stem from popular term paper topics, like capital punishment, and personal circumstances, like choosing a college, finding a job, and buying a home. One way to help people with these predictable requests is to create pathfinders, or written guides, that help library users find useful information.

### From Paper to the Web

Librarians have been producing pathfinders on paper for many years. Increasingly, paper pathfinders are giving way to World Wide Web guides. Using the Web has many advantages. Web-based guides are available to remote users as well as to those who are in the library. As more and more of our reference resources are on the World Wide Web, Web-based guides not only list the best sources, but also provide direct access to them. Similarly, as library catalogs and periodicals databases increasingly move to the Web, pathfinders that list library books, articles, or search terms can be linked directly to the sources

Another major advantage of Web-based pathfinders is that they can be easily and instantly updated. Many academic libraries used to produce library guides for their bibliographic instruction programs, only to find that new releases and new options made these guides out of date as soon as they were printed. After years of pleading with vendors and systems administrators not to make any changes during the semester, many libraries have moved all guides to the library's Web pages, where they can be updated as needed and printed just before an instruction session—if they are printed at all.

The Morris County (N.J.) Library's reference department has an interesting collection of pathfinders on their Web page (*www.gti.net/mocolib1/ref.html*). These are practical guides to some of the most common situations that send people to the public library looking for information. All of the guides integrate several types of information: for example, links to recommended Web resources, information on print and other reference works available in the library, and information on state agencies or other organizations that can offer assistance.

The Endangered Species page (*www.gti.net/mocolib1/species.html*), for example, includes a list of helpful reference books, a list of relevant subject headings for searching the library catalog, and links to Web sites. The pathfinder for Company Information (*www.gti.net/mocolib1/company.html*) provides a helpful, well-organized selection of resources (primarily Web resources), with links to New Jersey resources. There is also a message that is both explicitly stated and implicit through the whole, helpful page: "Ask your librarian!"

One of Morris County's guides, called Helping Your Elders (*www.gti.net/mocolib1/elders.html*), is aimed at those who are caring for elderly parents (Figure 7–1). As this guide notes, "There can be too much to think about at once if you suddenly have to help an elderly relation change his or her life style or situation." This page brings together different types of information that may be needed. In addition to the obvious subjects, such as Social Security and nursing homes, it also has pointers for those selling a car or needing to value art and other possessions.

Colleges and university libraries, with a long history of bibliographic instruction programs, are also active in creating pathfinders and other types of guides for their students and other library users. Sometimes the most useful guides are the most basic, including the University of Pittsburgh's guide called simply Finding Stuff (*www.pitt.*

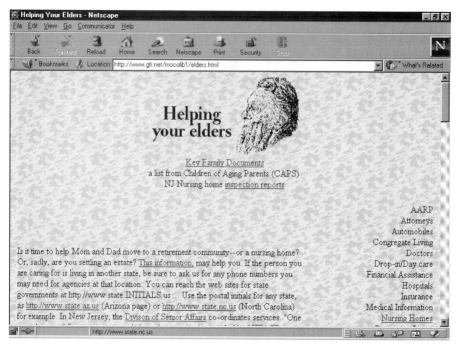

**Figure 7–1. Helping Your Elders—A Reference Pathfinder from the Morris County Library.**

*edu/~refquest/LI/Finding_Stuff.html*). With links to more specific guides, this introduction to library research provides basic information on the library, the location of material by call numbers, the library hours, and so on.

The Informatics Center of Vanderbilt University Medical Center, maintains the Active Digital Library (*www.mc. vanderbilt.edu/adl/pathfinders/*), a collection of excellent pathfinders on different aspects of HIV/AIDS. A good example is Care of the Caregiver (*www.mc. vanderbilt.edu/ adl/pathfinders/caregiver/*), by Jim Gibson of the School of Nursing. It includes lists of selected books, journals, local organizations, and electronic resources. Although this guide is prepared to support Vanderbilt's HIV/AIDS Outreach Project, having it on the World Wide Web makes it a valuable resource for a much wider audience.

### Class Project Pathfinders

Some libraries are now producing custom pathfinders for class projects. The Technology Center of the Lakewood (Ohio) Public Library (*www.lkwdpl.org/techctr.htm*) works with local teachers to produce pathfinders for class assignments. Teachers submit pathfinder requests, describing the assignment and type of resources that should be included. They may suggest specific sites, but most of the research and selection is done by the librarians. The Lakewood librarians feel that the time spent preparing the pathfinders is well worth it, since it allows them to be prepared for the assignment. Systems librarian Mary Ellen Stasek notes, "It is rather like self-defense with large classes working on a project."

The Technology Center prepares pathfinders for all levels. A first-grade pathfinder on penguins (*www.lkwdpl.org/schools/taft/penguins.htm*) is simple and colorful, and, at the request of the teacher, includes some links to other young students' projects (Figure 7–2). The library prepared an extensive guide for the middle school students preparing for the National History Day projects (*www.lkwdpl.org/schools/emerson/migrate.htm*), integrating information on many types of library resources in addition to the World Wide Web sources (Figure 7–3). A high school teacher worked with the library staff in a summer teacher camp to produce Mrs. Salipante's Foreign Food Recipes (*www.*

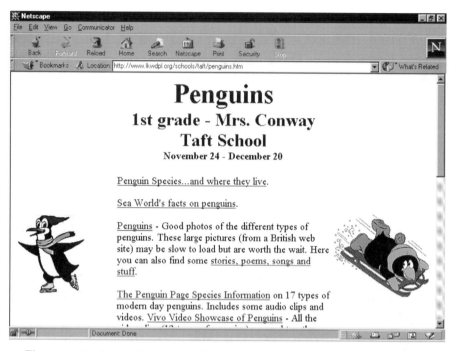

**Figure 7–2. Penguins—A Pathfinder for a First Grade Class from the Technology Center of the Lakewood Public Library.**

*lkwdpl.org/lhs/foreignfoods/*) for the students in her Gourmet Foods class (Figure 7–4).

The Lakewood librarians find that the class pathfinders are appreciated in different ways by teachers, parents, and students. Mary Ellen Stasek says that:

> . . . when teachers point students to the Web, they prefer there be some direction or roadmap for research. They are less comfortable making the assignment when the kids are poking about blindly. Many parents that have Internet access at home still lack confidence in their searching skills and are glad to have a

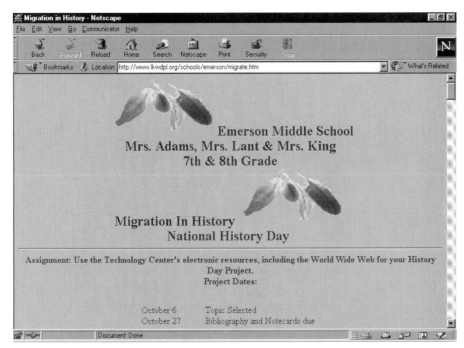

**Figure 7–3. Migration in History—A National History Day Pathfinder from the Technology Center of the Lakewood Public Library.**

clear path to follow. Parents that come to the library with children often express amazement at the wealth and variety of material available. The children think it's kind of neat going to "my teacher's page." They take the information for granted (Stasek, 1998).

### Beyond Libraries

Librarians are not the only ones organizing World Wide Web resources. Many groups produce Web guides that are not unlike library pathfinders. Yahoo! does an outstanding job with its Full Coverage pages on special events

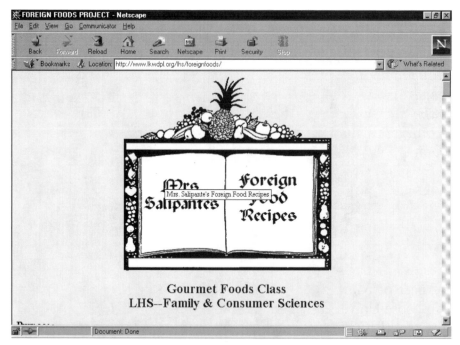

**Figure 7–4. Mrs. Salipante's Foreign Food—A Class Pathfinder from the Technology Center of the Lakewood Public Library.**

(*headlines.yahoo.com/Full_Coverage/*). They produce these pages for many current events topics, and update them frequently. Topics for the pages include not only political events, but also various kinds of disasters, deaths of prominent people, major trials, sports events, and, perhaps most useful for reference work, ongoing issues like cloning, global warming, and breast cancer research.

Full Coverage pages provide direct links to selected, high-interest articles from newspapers and journals, sound and video files from CNN, the BBC, NPR, and other broadcasting sites; local newspaper Web sites or other sources of continuing, in-depth coverage; Web sites providing background information; to related Yahoo categories. These pages make it easy to link quickly to the best coverage of a topic or event, and make it easy to gather different points of view. For example, the Full Coverage page on the Northern Ireland Peace Process (*headlines. yahoo.com/Full_Coverage/World/Northern_Ireland_ Conflict/*) includes links to the *Belfast Telegraph*, the *Irish Times*, and the BBC.

### Special Projects

Some librarians create specialized resources designed for reference services. One of the best-known of these is The Best Information on the Net (*www.sau.edu/bestinfo/*), a project of Marylaine Block of the O'Keefe Library at St. Ambrose University (Figure 7–5). The Best Information on the Net (BIOTN) is a masterpiece of space planning, written in a very concise, table format to provide the maximum number of useful and well-organized links with a minimum of clicking and scrolling. Block thoughtfully includes a large-type version for those who find her format a little *too* concise.

Block provides links to all sorts of general reference information, including a special set of links for faculty and administration. One of the most useful features is something that perhaps only a reference librarian could have done: a Hot Paper Topics index (with collections of links on Affirmative Action, Death Penalty, Gun Control, Welfare Reform, and so on), along with Help for Term Paper Writers and Avoiding Plagiarism. The reference desk section is organized in a particularly useful and intuitive manner (with topics like How Do I Say It?, What Is It?, Where Is It?, Who Is It?, and Who Said It?).

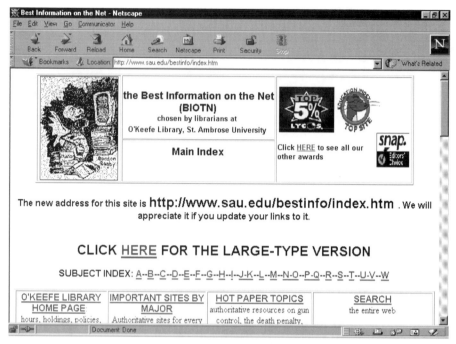

**Figure 7–5. BIOTN: The Best Information on the Net, from the O'Keefe Library at St. Ambrose University.**

Gary Price of the German Library, George Washington University, has developed a special collection of links that is of great benefit to reference librarians and their clients. Price's List of Lists (*gwis2.circ.gwu.edu/~gprice/listof.htm*) is an organized collection of links to various lists available on various World Wide Web sites (Figure 7–6). Most of these are lists from various periodical, government, and association Web sites, including such things as the Top 100 PR Agencies from PR Central, the top-grossing films of all time from *Variety*, the 250 richest towns in America from *Worth*, and the Fortune 500. Gary Price maintains another useful site, Direct Search (*gwis2.circ.gwu.edu/~gprice/*

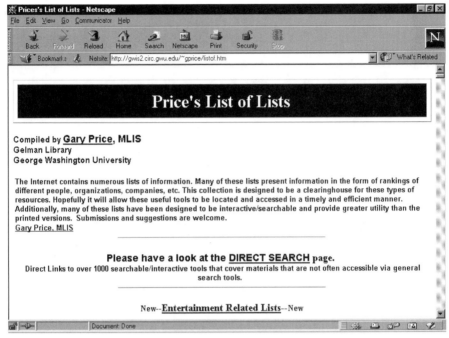

**Figure 7–6. Price's List of Lists—A Project of Gary Price.**

*direct.htm*), which provides direct access to the various searchable databases on the Web (Figure 7–7).

Creative librarians like Marylaine Block and Gary Price develop special guides for the users of their own libraries, but once these are published on the World Wide Web, they are also available to the rest of us—to use, and to inspire us to develop our own tools.

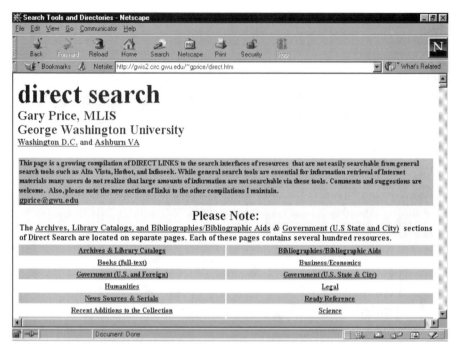

Figure 7–7. Direct Search—A Project of Gary Price

## PARTNERSHIPS

Some libraries have expanded their role within the community; they not only provide access to information, but help organizations within the community to organize and present their own information resources on the World Wide Web.

The Technology Center of the Lakewood (Ohio) Public Library provides Web services not only for the library, but also for the city government, the schools, and many non-profit groups. Mary Ellen Stasek, the system librarian, writes, "We are striving to be the prime information source for our community .... We seek to expand our scope from collecting and organizing to publishing and disseminating" (Stasek, 1998).

The library uses the power of hyperlinking to enhance their community Web sites with connections to relevant information sources. For example, on the Web page for the local community theatre, Beck Center for the Performing Arts (*www.lkwdpl.org/beck/*), there are links to Web sites related to the playwrights whose works are being performed.

The library also produces a Web site for an organization called Women in History (*www.lkwdpl.org/wihohio/*) that performs dramatic recreations of the lives of notable American women. For this site, the library has developed individual biographical pages for many of the women featured in the performances, with biographical information, recommended reading, and links to other sites.

According to Stasek, these projects are "a natural outgrowth of the librarian's inclination to gather and group. . . . Our use of technology to enhance traditional library service is only limited by time and cost(!), not by desire or imagination" (Stasek, 1998).

In Maryland, Baltimore County Public Library provides Internet services to nonprofit organizations through a project called InfoLink (*www.bcpl.lib.md.us/commpg/ infolink/infolink.html*). For a low annual fee, the nonprofit gets dial-in access to the Internet with e-mail and Web site hosting, training, and technical support. The nonprofits get easy and inexpensive access to the Internet, with support from an organization that they know and trust, the library continues filling its mission to provide information services to the community, and the people of Baltimore County benefit from the availability of more local information on the World Wide Web.

The Three Rivers Free-Net (*trfn.clpgh.org*), a service of
the Carnegie Library of Pittsburgh, brings local nonprofit
and government organizations onto the Web by providing e-mail and Web site services, including training and
support, at no charge. These organizations become Information Providers (or IPs) for the Free-Net, and they are
encouraged to use their sites not only to provide information about their own organization and its services, but to
select links to follow-up or complementary services in their
field. This linking has not only made it easier for area residents to find appropriate services; it has also made the organizations more familiar with each other, and helped
them to identify duplications and gaps in service.

The Three Rivers Free-Net was one of the first community networks to be sponsored by a public library, but it's
a natural alliance. Susan F. Holmes, the project manager
for the Free-Net, believes that librarians brought special
strengths to the project. Their experiences in meeting informational needs of library users have helped them work
with the information provided to determine what information to present on their sites and how it can be organized.

In addition, the library's sponsorship has played a major role in attracting the IPs to come build their sites on
the Free-Net. The library's traditional role has helped
TRFN develop as a resource where the interests of all
members of the community can be represented. (Holmes,
1998).

## FIVE STRATEGIES FOR SUCCESS

This is a time of great change in the world of information, and reference librarians need to respond by keeping up with what's going on, providing guidance to our library users, and looking for new opportunities to connect people with the information they need.

1. Provide a variety of training opportunities for reference staff members.
   All reference staff members need regular training to improve their knowledge and skills, but they don't necessarily all need the same kinds of training. Encourage people to help develop their own training plans, with a combination of training sessions and self-directed learning that works for each individual. Meet regularly to plan and discuss training experiences and share what has been learned.

2. Plan a variety of ways to provide training and guidance for library users.
   Some people like to come to the library for training sessions, some want individual help at workstations, and others benefit more from written material, including guides to different services and pathfinders on particular subjects.

3. In all training situations, build on existing interests and strengths.
   People learn more when new material is specific, practical, and anchored to their personal interests. This is why subject-based Internet training is usually more

successful than general introductory sessions, and why one-on-one help, when the patron is directly engaged in a particular project, may be the most useful of all.

4. Develop pathfinders that combine different types of resources.
   Our libraries have many different types of resources: reference and circulating books, periodical articles, Internet resources, and more, all of which generally need to be searched separately. When librarians develop guides combining different types of resources for high-interest topics, we are helping people learn about the full range of resources available.

5. Develop partnerships with other groups in your community.
   Librarians have the skills and experience of connecting people with all kinds of information. We can extend that role through creative partnerships with other groups in the community, cooperating on everything from reading lists to the creation of Web sites.

This is a time of great opportunity, but with everything changing so quickly, it's sometimes difficult for librarians to keep a step ahead of our library users. We need cooperation and planning to ensure that staff members get adequate time and support for training and independent learning, and to ensure that they share what they learn. We also need planning to provide our library users with different kinds of training and support so they can use library resources more effectively.

# Chapter 8

# Statistics Can Help
# Ensure Quality

Reference librarians are in the business of providing information to people, and we often must do this quickly, while the patron is standing there or is still on the phone. We find an answer and give it to the patron, but how do we know how accurate or helpful that information is? If the patron asked the same question of three different libraries, or of three different librarians at the same library, would he or she get three different answers?

How do our library users see the service that we deliver? After a reference encounter, do they feel that we were as interested in their question and as helpful as we could be? Will they return to us and recommend our services to others?

And how much service are we actually delivering? Most of us feel that we are busier than ever, and that we need more staff to cover the desk, answer the phones, help patrons at workstations; we also feel we need more time away from the desk to be receiving training, doing bibliographic instruction, and working on special projects. How can we measure the amount of service that we are giving? Is it enough to just count reference questions anymore?

These are some of the issues that reference librarians and library administrators must deal with as we try to measure and evaluate reference services. We need a combination of quantitative factors (how much? how many?) and qualitative factors (how good?) to form a true picture of our reference services. We need this kind of information so that we can continuously try to develop and improve our services and thus better fulfill the needs of our communities.

## COUNTING

For many decades, libraries relied on the most basic form of statistics in order to measure services. We counted things. We counted the number of items that were checked out of the library and we counted the number of questions that we answered. As libraries became involved in providing programs, we counted attendance.

Over time, we looked for ways to quantify services that might be missed by the things we were already counting. What about people who came to the library and spent time using our material, but didn't check anything out or ask any questions? Many libraries added people-counting devices to library entrances so that we could track how many people came into the library, whether or not they borrowed material, and many libraries developed systems for counting in-house use of material, usually by counting items that needed reshelving at the end of the day.

Most organizations use counts of various types as output measures—sales figures, for example. But output measures can be problematic, especially in a service as complex as reference, and such counts need to implemented and interpreted with care.

Selecting an output measure is a tricky business, because whatever we decide to count as a measure of activity tends to become the activity that is seen as the most important. What we count, counts. Consciously or unconsciously, we tend to focus on those figures, and to interpret higher figures as a measure of success, and lower ones as a problem. This tendency can interfere with the motivation to improve service rather than improve our statistics.

Most libraries count reference questions. This is not as simple a matter as output measures in many businesses, like the number of shirts pressed or bagels sold. Do simple, factual questions, like "Who is my Representative in Congress?" count the same as more complicated questions that require some research and synthesis to produce a useful answer? And what about questions like "Where's *Writer's Market*?" Or even, "Where's the pay phone?"

In order to make reference statistics more meaningful, many libraries separate types of questions. It's common to have a separate category for "directional" questions, which takes care of the pay phone, but is the *Writer's Market* question directional? Does directional mean just giving physical directions, like "down the hall, and through the doorway to your left," or does it include giving a call number or taking a patron to the shelf to locate a book? And if you offer help to the patron in using *Writer's Market* or direct that person to related resources, has that directional question become a real reference question?

Libraries that separate directional from reference questions usually have some kind of guidelines for how to count these, but it gets complicated. If a patron asks who were the Union and Confederate generals at the Battle of Gettysburg, is that one reference question or two? Is it one if the patron asks for both at once, and two if the patron asks for one and then comes back to the desk ten minutes later to ask for the other?

And how do we count all of the interactions with people that aren't exactly questions? Many reference librarians report spending less time providing answers to questions, and much more time assisting users with various electronic resources. This might mean starting someone off with a search, and then going back over to the workstation three times to answer questions and demonstrate some advanced searching techniques. Is that one question or four?

In a library with a small staff and little turnover, with only a few people involved in reference, it's relatively easy to agree on guidelines for how to count various types of questions. But in larger libraries and those with many people covering reference, including part-time and week-end staff and a lot of staff turnover, the method of keeping reference statistics may vary considerably from shift to shift. Many libraries have one staff member who is notorious for inflated statistics, counting every little thing he or she does, and another who has the opposite tendency and either forgets or chooses not to bother to count most encounters. And even when all librarians agree on how to record statistics for different types of questions, actually remembering to mark them all down is a problem. During slow periods, when there is a break between patrons, all questions may be recorded, but during busy shifts, when a trip across the reference room may result in helping several people, librarians may have trouble remembering and recording all transactions.

Systems of recording and cumulating these statistics also vary. In some libraries, statistics are simply kept by making marks on a pad of paper, counting these up daily, and cumulating the totals weekly, monthly, and annually. Better information can be gained from statistics if they are more detailed, so that the variations between different times of day can be reported. If libraries not only count the number of times they help people using workstations, but which resources they worked with, more information can be gained. If a large percentage of time is spent assisting patrons at a particular database, that may suggest the need for better training aids or for changes in workstation or software options to make things easier. However, the more detailed the statistics, the greater burden it is to try to keep them accurately.

All of these variations in how reference statistics are kept mean that managers cannot rely too heavily on these statistics when comparing reference activity from one year to the next or when making decisions about appropriate staffing levels. It also means that when these statistics are gathered from different libraries and compared, false impressions may be created. Reference statistics are not without value, but they must be examined in context, and as reflecting only one aspect of the department's work.

## FEWER QUESTIONS, BETTER SERVICE

Some of the most valuable work of reference librarians improves service but may lower the number of questions that come across the reference desk and get counted. Improvements in the design of the reference area and the library as a whole can cause a dramatic decrease in the number of directional questions. Signs, handouts, guides, newsletters, pathfinders, training sessions, and similar activities can be viewed as preventative reference—they answer many questions before they become questions.

Sometimes a simple change, like putting a dictionary in a prominent location, can make a big difference. Reference librarians need to look beyond what the numbers are to what the questions are, and look for types of questions that could be reduced (by making high-demand items easier to find) or made easier and less time-consuming to answer (by providing guides, in paper or online, for common questions).

Improvements to the circulating nonfiction collection, so that patrons can easily find books on subjects of interest, can also reduce the number of reference questions. Many patrons come to the reference desk for help in finding information only after finding nothing on the shelf to check out. Reference librarians should be actively involved with collection development, since they have valuable information on what topics are not adequately covered in the circulating collection.

Great improvements can often be made to service by duplicating popular titles on important topics, with the goal that the library always have certain material available for circulation. In public libraries, it's especially important to have adequate material on health topics. If a patron is looking for information on a particular health issue, he or she cannot wait for two or three weeks until material is returned. Reference works are some help, but a poor substitute for a few good books that can be taken home. In many libraries, the reference area is swamped with students doing predictable projects on Ancient Egypt, explorers, inventors, presidents, and so on. The first few students who arrive check out all the circulating books, and the rest of the students spend hours at the library using reserve or reference material. It's often a good investment in service to buy multiple copies of the most popular titles, let the students take them home, and store them if necessary until the next assignment onslaught.

## NEW STATISTICS

As more and more resources become electronic, and as libraries support remote access to reference databases, libraries are looking for new things to count. Like so many other things in the Information Age, however, the possibilities are endless but never simple.

For example, many libraries have full-text periodical databases available in some online format. These services may be replacing, to a large extent, the more traditional service of having collections of back issues of periodicals, with indexes to provide access. Libraries could count the periodicals that were used—by circulation statistics, paging slips, or similar methods. These statistics were primitive, but they were easy to understand and to compare from month to month and year to year.

Electronic products often compile and report a variety of statistics, including the number of sessions, the number of searches, the number of hits, the number of full-text articles retrieved, and the number of articles printed, downloaded, or e-mailed. Which of these statistics is useful to us?

The number of sessions usually reflects the number of times a product is used, assuming that the system initiates a new session for each user. During busy times, this may not happen, when a group of students perform searches one after the other without exiting. The number of searches is interesting, but what does it mean? If the number of searches is two or three times as high as the number of sessions, does it mean that users are performing two or three different searches? Or does it mean that users are doing a search, looking at the results, and then refining the search? And if it does mean that most users take two or three tries for each search, is that a problem, or just a search technique?

The number of hits, or citations retrieved, can be an interesting number, but do high numbers mean that users are getting access to a lot of material (which is good) or that they are being drowned in irrelevant hits (which is bad)?

The statistics from electronic products can also change dramatically when new releases or different options are selected. For example, the number of citations retrieved might drop dramatically if an option is turned on to limit the default search to articles available in full-text or longer than one page. These changes might lower the statistics but improve service by presenting a smaller but better selection of hits.

Some of the most interesting statistics are those for the remote users—those connecting to library resources from home, school, or office. For licensed databases supporting home access, there is usually some method of validation, often using the student identification number or library barcode, which helps gather good statistics. But how do you count use of the library's World Wide Web page? You can get hits, but can you distinguish between people in your own community (who are likely using your library's resources) and people from around the world (who may just stumble across your page and spend only seconds viewing it to determine that it is irrelevant)?

It's difficult to interpret some of these statistics, but gathering and discussing them can be interesting. Here are some points that you may want to consider:

- Make sure that you read the documentation and talk to systems people if necessary to understand what statistics are being gathered, and what is and isn't included.
- If the statistics are not what you need, see if the system can be changed or adapted to collect the information that you want.
- Record the date of new releases or changes to configurations so that you can relate the change to any changes in statistics.
- Rely on your observation of how your patrons use different systems to interpret the meaning of statistics.

## ACCURACY

The idea that reference librarians are successful in answering questions only a little over half of the time has had profound effects in the field of librarianship. The research has been repeated and refined, respected and reviled . . . but it has never been ignored.

Outside of academe, reference librarians find these studies confusing and disturbing. We are confused by the high percentage of incorrect answers, and wonder how these could have occurred. Presumably, the librarians involved weren't guessing, or making up answers, so where did these wrong answers come from? Were reference librarians giving answers taken from the usual, well-respected reference resources, and it was these answers that were wrong? If so, is that a failure of the librarian or the publisher? What if the librarian gives a source, saying, for example, "According to the *World Book Encyclopedia*, the nickname for the wife of President Rutherford B. Hayes was 'Lemonade Lucy'"? If that fact is untrue, is the answer, in that form incorrect? Just how far should we go in verifying the accuracy of answers to factual questions?

Many librarians also have serious concerns about both the effectiveness and ethics of unobtrusive testing. If staff know that anyone they serve might be a tester rather than a real patron, will this affect their ability to give appropriate service? Is it possible that in trying not to "fail," librarians might overload patrons with information they don't really want or need?

Libraries are not the only organizations with an accuracy problem. In February, 1998, Hank Phillippi Ryan, the Consumer Reporter for WHDH-TV, broadcast a report called "Who Ya Gonna Call?" testing several different Massachusetts state agency telephone hotlines. The questions were simple, factual ones. The Consumer Affairs agency was tested with questions taken directly from the FAQs on their own Web site and the Registry of Motor Vehicles was asked questions from the driver's manual. Although some departments did well, others did so poorly that the investigators were given the wrong answer almost half of the time—it may be that the "55 Percent Rule" applies beyond librarianship. The report ends by noting that when directors of these agencies were told the results of Ryan's experiment in unobtrusive testing, they said that if someone receives the wrong information, they want to know about it. "But," Ryan notes, "here's another question they couldn't get right: how are you supposed to know when an answer is wrong?" (Ryan, 1998).

This is the question that troubles reference librarians about the 55 Percent Rule. If the information that we dispense is not accurate, will patrons know? Will they eventually discover that fact and blame us, or will they rely on that information, and possibly be harmed in some way? For people who devote their professional lives to helping people with their information needs, these are troubling questions.

Some of the troubling things about the unobtrusive testing is that it uses brief, factual questions, a type of question that typically makes up one quarter or less of a library's patron interactions. Even libraries who have only a 55 percent success rate on these questions may have a much higher rate of overall success for all types of patrons. Many librarians also feel that the testing situation is false— the proxies who are asking questions are not typical patrons, do not have any personal motivation for seeking the answers to the question they are asking, and can't give real feedback to the librarian who is trying to serve them.

A great advantage of unobtrusive testing, however, is the fact that it tests service as it is usually given—without the self-consciousness of a testing situation, which may cause some staff members to perform at a better level than they usually do and others to become nervous and underperform.

Other researchers report on projects that measure user satisfaction, rather than accuracy of answers. One such project at the Central Missouri State University successfully combined the use of unobtrusive testing and user satisfaction. Senior-level marketing research students, under the guidance of their professor and representatives of the library, undertook this project as a case study, with the library as the client. The students were trained in the theories and problems of conducting subjective surveys. In this test, the students did not ask factual questions, but requested help using the online catalog and a CD-ROM index to find books and articles on a particular topic. After their reference encounters, the students filled out questionnaires rating the staff member on several behaviors including "Approached me before I asked for help" and "Directed me to the right place instead of only pointing." The results of all of the students' reports were collected and tallied. Since it was the reference service itself that was being evaluated, there was no tracking of individual staff members, but results were broken down by time-of-day. The quantitative measurements from these questionnaires was supplemented by focus group conversations and written reports. The information from this study was a candid evaluation of reference services from the point-of-view of students (Tygett, Lawson, and Weessies, 1996).

Another major way of evaluating reference services is through the use of user satisfaction surveys. Libraries ask patrons to fill out the survey after receiving service, not unlike the way that hotels and restaurants commonly leave survey forms for guests. However, a more sophisticated method is that developed by Charles Bunge at the University of Wisconsin-Madison used by WOREP, the Wisconsin-Ohio Reference Evaluation Program. In the WOREP program, the patron is told that the library is conducting a survey and is given a survey form to be filled and deposited in a box away from the reference desk, while the librarian fills in a checklist for the transaction which can be matched with the patron's. The librarian's form can provide valuable information that supplements the patron's perception of success or failure. For example, librarians can indicate whether or not the reference area was busy during this encounter, limiting the amount of time they could spend with the patron, or if needed material was missing from the shelf or located in another department (Stalker and Murfin, 1996).

WOREP and other studies that rely on surveys of patron satisfaction have three advantages over the unobtrusive studies. The first is content validity: unlike the contrived factual questions asked by proxies, the survey studies measure the effectiveness of the staff in handling real, and presumably representative, questions and patrons. The second is context: the information recorded by the librarian and matched to the patron's survey form can give valuable information on the factors that are related to success and failure. The third is consensus: the library administration, staff and patrons are cooperating in the assessment process, without the trust and trickery issues that can surround the use of proxies.

Two disadvantages of this method should be noted. While the survey approach eliminates the violation of trust that many librarians feel accompanies the use of proxies, it does mean that librarians know that they are being going to be evaluated by patrons, which may affect their performance. The other disadvantage is that it places some of the burden for the evaluation on our busy patrons, who may not want to take the time to fill out a form or may feel uncomfortable making negative comments.


## ROOM FOR IMPROVEMENT

The purpose of evaluating reference service is to find ways to maintain and improve the quality of that service. However, the research seems unable to determine which factors lead to reference success. Collection size seems to have some effect, with collections in the medium range the most effective. The amount of time spent with the patron, the education of the librarian, and many other factors do not seem to have strong statistical correlation with accuracy.

Two key behaviors do seem to have a definite positive effect on reference success, both basic communication skills. The first is paraphrasing the patron's question, so that both have an understanding of what information is being sought. The second is soliciting feedback from the patron, by asking a question like, "Does this completely answer your question?" or, in the case of a patron who has been directed to some resources to work independently, "Are you finding what you need?" These two behaviors are essential skills; fortunately, both skills can be taught.

In 1983, Maryland's Division of Library Development and Services (DLDS) conducted an unobtrusive reference survey in 60 public libraries. The results of this survey indicated that Maryland's reference librarians were giving full and complete answers just 55 percent of the time. From the information learned in the project, the staff developed a list of 23 model reference behaviors that seemed to improve the results of a reference interaction, and began a training program to teach the use of these skills to representatives from library systems across the state, who would then conduct training within their own systems.

In 1986, the DLDS repeated the unobtrusive survey in the same 60 public libraries. The survey confirmed that the use of the model reference behaviors had a significant impact on the quality of reference service. Those librarians who had been trained in the use of the behaviors were successful 77 per cent of the time. The DLDS conducted more training, using a train the trainer approach, for the state's library systems (Isenstein, 1992, p. 35).

It is not difficult to talk about the importance of some new set of behaviors, or to demonstrate it in training. What is tough is getting people to try the new behaviors on the job, and to replace entrenched habits with new ones. This is a challenge in any workplace situation, but especially so in reference, where the pace is fast and the situations varied. It's relatively easy, for example, for a restaurant to train a new interviewing technique to waiters and waitresses, anticipating all situations that are likely to arise as customers order. But for librarians, the situation is much more complicated, since reference is a place where everything is on the menu. It takes time and coaching to learn how to apply the techniques, especially open questioning and verifying, in real life situations.

Baltimore County Public Library was one of the Maryland systems that received this training and put it into practice in its branches, through a program called STAR: System Training for Accurate Reference. The STAR trainers decided to focus on the three most significant model behaviors: the use of open questions, verifying the patron's request, and asking follow-up questions. All professional librarians and paraprofessionals received one full day of training with a half day follow up three weeks later.

To help Baltimore County's librarians learn to apply the techniques, the library instituted a system of peer coaching. Pairs of librarians worked together two or three times a week, with one partner observing a reference encounter of the other, recording the use of the techniques for later discussion. This gave every staff member many opportunities to practice the new behaviors and receive feedback in a variety of circumstances. After over a year of training and peer coaching, the use of the model reference behaviors was incorporated into the formal performance review process (Isenstein, 1992).

Learning how to conduct a proper reference interview will ensure that the librarian understands the question, but the other element of reference success is knowing how and where to find the answers. We have already discussed the need for formal training, but there is another evaluation method that can be very useful—group evaluation. This is the method as described in the manual of the Reference Evaluation Project of the North Suburban Library System:

> This technique combines evaluation and training in which all staff in a department work independently to answer the same set of factual questions in a given period of time. The answers are then evaluated and discussed at a meeting of the group. If the staff mem-

bers have the opportunity to discuss sources, strategies and techniques in answering the questions, this method of evaluation, if used periodically, can serve as a development aid for both new and experienced staff (North Suburban Library Association, 1992).

There are many variations of this method. For example, the staff can look at the questions together and discuss where and how they would look for answers before they actually make the attempt. This is a good way to develop the instinct for where an answer might be found.

Another possibility is to examine and discuss a group of questions and answers from another source—for example, from Frequently Asked Questions files from the World Wide Web, from library or other Web sites. The staff can discuss the answers given and decide whether they are accurate, objective, and complete. Librarians might then follow up on these questions to develop a better answer. This has the advantage of helping the staff focus on an element that goes a step beyond accuracy, that of completeness.

These group discussions of reference questions help move training from the classroom into the library itself, and librarians can learn a great deal from hearing how others approach different types of questions. This is more important now than ever, since the Internet and other electronic resources have brought so many additional choices to our libraries.

There's another reason why these sessions can be helpful. They give librarians a chance to discuss answers—accurate or not, adequate or otherwise—in a supportive atmosphere. One of the most difficult aspects of reference evaluation is that librarians want to give good service, try to give good service, and are very uncomfortable discussing errors made with real patron inquiries. Discussing practice questions allows librarians to share ideas and experiences honestly, without worrying about failure.

Sometimes these discussions reveal that some staff members use different methods to find answers. Some people, for example, often telephone a local expert or another organization to get answers. The staff can discuss when this is appropriate and when it isn't.

## FOCUS GROUPS

Many libraries, especially academic libraries, also use focus groups to evaluate reference and other services. A focus group involves bringing together a group representing the library's community to discuss different aspects of library services and how they feel about them. The group is usually led by a professional facilitator, who is skilled in drawing out the opinions of the participants, using open questions. The facilitator follows an agenda to make sure basic issues are discussed, but with enough flexibility to allow the group to develop its own ideas.

The library has many different groups of users, and the library may use mixed focus groups that include representatives of all groups, or separate sessions for different groups like undergraduate students, graduate students, and faculty. Focus groups are generally drawn from the library's whole community, including those who use the library infrequently or not at all. These people can provide valuable insights into groups the library is not reaching.

Focus groups can reveal the preferences and priorities of library users, and provide valuable information for discussion and planning. Sometimes focus groups are combined with other survey methods. For example, the Duke University Library conducted a series of focus groups and used information from those sessions to define issues for a survey to be sent to a much larger segment of the community. Focus groups are good for getting qualitative information, and surveys are good for getting quantitative information.

Focus groups can also provide some insights, suggestions, and information on problems that can be addressed immediately. It is common for a focus group to lead to greater efforts in signage, user aids, and public relations. This often happens when focus group attendees say they wish the library would introduce collections and services which it already has.

## FIVE STRATEGIES FOR SUCCESS

In the constant pressure of daily service, and the increasing need to plan for quickly evolving new services, we sometimes neglect to measure and examine the results of all our plans and activities.

1. Count questions, but make sure everyone knows what you're counting and why.
   Keeping a tally of reference questions can be useful, but only if all staff members understand the system and follow the same standards. This requires clear guidelines, training, and reminders. The staff won't

take these statistics seriously, however, unless they see
that they are used to plan staffing levels and make
other changes to improve service.

2. Develop meaningful measures of other reference services.
   What else can you count? Everything—attendance at
   training sessions for patrons, use of computer workstations and different databases, use of microfilm, reference pathfinders developed or updated, just about
   anything that you do—can be logged and tallied.
   Work with all members of the reference staff and administration to develop useful measures of activity. But
   don't count things unless you are going to look at the
   numbers over time, and use them for planning and
   evaluation.

3. Look at things from the patron's point of view and
   practice preventative reference.
   Sometimes the best reference service makes it unnecessary for people to spend time in the library using
   reference material. Consider adding circulating copies of popular reference works. Look at those directional questions and see if you can develop better
   signage and library guides to help people find their
   way around on their own.

4. Develop methods to measure the accuracy and quality of reference service.
   The reference staff and library administration should
   work together to develop methods of evaluating reference service. Surveys, supervisor or peer observation,

or the use of proxies may be included. Evaluation should include all types of service and no trick questions.

Reference librarians are less apt to be resistant to such evaluation efforts if they become a regular, ongoing part of the library program, than if they are seen as some new management fad.

5. Focus on improving service, not fixing blame.
All evaluation activities should have the clear goal of improving service. Seek ways to develop an honest, trustful atmosphere within the reference department and the library as a whole so that evaluation is seen as a cooperative venture that helps librarians provide better service.

# Chapter 9

# World Wide Web:
# Challenges and Opportunities

In less than a decade, the Internet has gone from a set of resources and protocols almost unknown outside college and computing circles, to becoming a part of everyday life. It seems that every company, every product, every organization prominently displays its URL, and that no matter what you are interested in, there is at least one Web site devoted to the topic.

The World Wide Web is the subject of countless books, magazines, e-mail groups, classes, and, of course, Web sites. For many people, it's a source of information and entertainment, much like watching television or visiting the library. For others, it has become more than that, because on the Web it's easy to move beyond looking at other people's pages and into developing your own. It's an egalitarian medium, where anyone can in effect become a self-publisher, with very little investment in money or programming skills.

Self-publishing on the Web has many advantages over self-publishing in print, where a document must be prepared, duplicated, and distributed. On the Web, a document is prepared and made available, but is duplicated and distributed on the fly, when others connect to it via the Web. This not only makes self-publishing on the Web economical; it means that a modest beginning can grow and develop and be endlessly edited and improved.

The major publishing issue on the Web is not getting a page set up in the first place, but letting other people know that it's there. Publicity is usually accomplished by sending announcements to e-mail groups, newsgroups, and Web sites devoted to related subjects. In many cases, Web sites actually grow out of the developer's involvement and postings to subject-oriented e-mail groups and newsgroups.

It's often said that print publications are generally of higher quality than Web publications because of the selective filtering process that publishers provide. However, there is a selective filtering process on the World Wide Web as well—it just happens after the fact rather than beforehand, and like so many things on the Web, it is a populist rather than centralized process. When a new site is announced, it enters into a competition for attention. If there is something particularly useful or interesting about the site, it will be noticed and mentioned in various forums, and the feedback from visitors generally leads to the improvement and growth of the site. Many modest single-page efforts develop into substantial, multipage Web sites over time, while many others die a natural death or languish for months or years without updating—becoming what are known as "cobweb sites."

The World Wide Web's rapid expansion and acceptance has been compared to the revolutionary changes in society brought about by radio in the 1920s and television in the 1950s. Radio and television were similar to the World Wide Web because they brought previously unimaginable experiences in sight and sound directly into the home; they combined news, information, education, and entertainment; they appealed to the interests of all members of the family, including children; and they combined programming and commercial sponsorship in complex and sometimes problematic ways.

The World Wide Web differs from radio and television, however, in one major way. Radio and television are broadcast media, in which control is centralized in a small number of producers and everyone else participates as part of the audience. On the World Wide Web (and other Internet services), however, everything is decentralized, and people participate in a much more interactive manner, whether it's by "surfing" at will, without the restrictions of broadcast schedules, or by developing their own Web-based resources.

In a time of booming growth and public enthusiasm for the concept of the Information Superhighway, it is perhaps ironic that librarians, especially reference librarians, who are perhaps the ultimate information professionals, are often more skeptical and less enthusiastic about the Internet than the general public. There are many reasons for this, all having to do with our unique relationship to information.

- Librarians work in libraries, and have much better access to information every day than other people. Often the information that other people are so thrilled with uncovering for themselves over the Internet is information that is readily available in standard reference sources that we are not only familiar with, but have at hand every day. We sometimes forget that the little information errands we can do on our coffee break (like looking up a health condition, the address of an organization, or consumer product reviews) require a special trip to the library for most people.

- This is a work skill for us, not a hobby. While other people are at home, surfing the Web for pleasure, we are trying diligently to master the skills needed to serve not only our own needs, but to help and instruct our library users. This tension can make us feel threatened and defensive. It also makes us feel incompetent, a feeling that is particularly difficult for reference librarians, who are accustomed to feeling very competent and knowledgeable. We are trying to manage ever-increasing numbers of public PCs, which bring with them a host of problems: pornography, printer jams, and scheduling, for example. These resource management issues don't always leave us much time or enthusiasm for discovery and training.
- Reference librarians are almost always seeking information for other people, not for themselves. While home users can take the time to explore resources related to three or four of their own special areas of interest, we are constantly jumping from topic to topic under time pressure. This difference makes it easy for home users to explore a limited set of resources and feel confident and comfortable with them, and difficult for librarians to feel the same way.
- Reference librarians have authority issues that are not shared by most home users, who have a much more casual and uncritical attitude toward information in

all formats. We are accustomed to working with resources that we believe to be accurate, current, and
authoritative—works that we have selected after reading reviews. Web resources are not selected beforehand, and we need to learn new ways to evaluate these
sources of information on the fly.

- Librarians value order, and are used to maintaining
  an organized and orderly environment. We are used
  to working with a catalog and Library of Congress
  subject headings and other relatively stable tools. The
  World Wide Web is an inherently dynamic, constantly
  changing environment, not one that lends itself to traditional organization or cataloging.

## PUBLIC WORKSTATIONS

PCs, browsers, and World Wide Web sites are all designed
around one assumption—that a PC really is a *personal*
computer, and that it belongs to an owner who can configure it to his or her own preferences and identity and
have access to all files. This arrangement, of course, is not
the case with public workstations in our libraries. Trying
to run essentially personal systems in a public mode brings
about a host of problems related to security, maintenance,
and training.

Reference librarians have been managing equipment in
their departments for several years: photocopy machines,
microfilm reader/printers, stand-alone CD-ROM workstations. But all of these machines are relatively simple,
trouble-free devices compared to the current generation of
networked, multimedia PCs. Not only are the new PC

workstations inherently complex and troublesome in a public environment, but there are so many of them! It seems that however many workstations a library has, it needs just a few more to satisfy the demand—and a few more, and a few more . . .

For maintenance and troubleshooting, it's best to be running a group of identical machines. In the volatile PC market, however, this is almost impossible to do unless all PCs are bought at once. A more typical situation is to have six PCs, bought over a period of six years, each with a slightly different combination of hardware and software.

Physical security of the equipment is the most basic problem that libraries face. There are a variety of ways to lock down the equipment, using security cables and other devices. But it's difficult to thwart the determined vandal or the truly careless. Some libraries have a problem with the theft of mouse balls, and have taken to checking them out from the desk, which is an inconvenience for both staff and patrons. Most libraries, even those that have coffee service somewhere in the building, prohibit food and drinks anywhere near the computer area, but some patrons still manage to spill sugar-laden drinks into the keyboards.

## SOUND

As sound has become increasingly important on the World Wide Web, libraries have either had to use speakers, which are disruptive to other patrons unless the PC is in a sound-proof enclosure of some kind, or use headphones, a device almost universally disliked by the library staff. Headphones are easy to steal or damage, and they raise some health and hygiene concerns in a public environment.

And yet, not having sound on public workstations means offering our patrons something less than the whole World Wide Web, which is inherently multimedia in nature. There are many Web sites where sounds are not an adjunct to print or graphical information; they are the information itself. Not having sound causes another problem in managing public workstations—since workstation utilization of sound is assumed by many Web site designers, patrons who click on sound file links or who hit pages that have background music may hang up the workstation with a series of error messages.

Sound on the World Wide Web is an example of how a single advance in technology can have a major impact on the way information is presented. In the early days of the World Wide Web, sound files had to be transferred from the host computer and then played by the PC. The size of sound files and the slowness of modems limited the practical length of sound files to small clips, often a minute or less. With the development of streaming audio and video technology, the situation changed dramatically. With streaming technology, once the beginning of a sound or video file is received the PC begins playing it. As the file is playing, the rest of the file is being received. This means that sound files can be many hours long. Streaming audio can also be used for real-time broadcasting, allowing users to watch CourtTV live (*www.courttv.com*) or listen to live radio stations from around the world through Quincy Jones's World Music site, Qradio (*www.qradio.net.*)

In addition to streaming audio, new sound formats have brought new promise and challenges to the World Wide Web. MPEG Layer 3, better known as MP3, provides high-quality, highly compressed sound files, which can easily

---

**Sometimes Hearing Is Believing: Five Sites with Sounds Too Good to Miss**

---

Sound is one of the hottest areas of development on the Web. Sound is the native format for many types of information: music, historic speeches, oral history, language study, and more. Here are some outstanding sites featuring sound files:

1. Music History 102: A Guide to Western Composers and Their Music from the Middle Ages to the Present
*www.ipl.org/exhibit/mushist/*

This outstanding educational site was created by Robert Sherrane, Cataloging Librarian of The Juilliard School, for the Internet Public Library. Music history text is beautifully complemented with sound files and artwork.

2. The Oyez Project: U.S. Supreme Court Multimedia Database
*oyez.nwu.edu*

This site, named for the phrase by which the marshal of the Supreme Court issues the call to order, includes recordings of the oral arguments for many important cases, along with links to the written opinions of the Court, biographies of the Supreme Court justices, and a variety of other resources. Hearing these arguments as they were delivered is quite a different experience from reading a few excerpts in casebooks.

3. NPR Online
*www.npr.org*

If you like National Public Radio on the air, you'll love it online. You can search this site or browse by program and date, and listen to entire programs or just the segment that you want.

   This is a great site to use to help a patron who is looking for the title of a book mentioned on the air. They've built up a substantial archives over the past few years, so searching this site for a particular topic can also turn up some interesting material—similar to searching a periodical index.

---

4. American Leaders Speak: Recordings from World War I and the 1920 Election, 1918–1920
*memory.loc.gov/ammem/nfhome.html*

Part of the American Memory Library of Congress's American Memory project, this is a meticulously documented, organized, and indexed collection of historic recordings, from Samuel Gompers to Calvin Coolidge. Photographs of the speakers and historical notes place each recording in context, and the written text accompanies each recording.

5. CD Now
*www.cdnow.com*

This online music store is an example of the blurring of distinctions between information and commerce on the World Wide Web. It's also a great resource for music reference. You can search by artist, album title, or song title, or browse by category. There are RealAudio sound clips for many of the songs—long enough to help identify a particular song. Partnership arrangements have added significant content, including reviews from *Rolling Stone* and *Billboard*. This site combines some of the best features of a music store, the Schwann catalog, and a stack of music magazines and reference books.

---

be created from compact discs and stored on the PC, transferred across the Internet, or played on small, offline MP3 players. The ease with which these files can be created and transferred is a matter of great concern to the music industry, who fear loss of revenue from the illegal distribution of copies of work protected by copyright. Secure formats and processes are being implemented to make it possible for music publishers, distributors, and performers to sell music directly to the consumer over the World Wide Web.

Now that file size is no longer a limitation, many sites

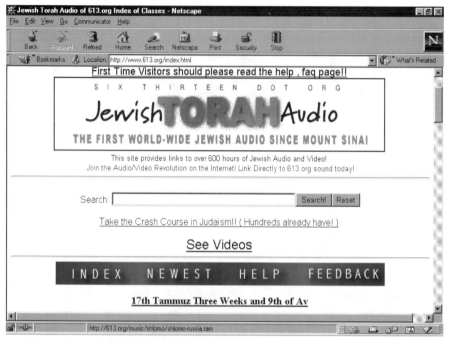

**Figure 9–1. Jewish Torah Audio.**

have developed collections of significant sound file archives. For example, the Jewish Torah Audio site (*www. 613.org*) describes itself as "the first world wide Jewish audio since Mount Sinai" and has a large collection including music, lessons, stories, and prayers (Figure 9–1). Streaming audio is used effectively here to convey both language and musical elements of Judaism that are difficult to convey in print.

Sites like Jewish Torah Audio are examples of how the World Wide Web can be used to bring important resource material to a much larger audience than would have ever had such access before. Such access, however, is only possible in libraries if we can deal with the added problems of managing speakers or headphones.

One promising approach to the problem is localized sound. The Virtual Audio Imager (*www.purestereo.com/brown.html*) is a system that mounts speakers in a dome that hangs overhead and effectively limits sound to a small area. Outside of the zone, sound levels drop by over 80 percent. These sound domes are in use in a number of cybercafes, information kiosks, and other businesses.

## SOFTWARE CHANGES

Most libraries also find it necessary to install some kind of security software or otherwise take steps to prevent patrons from making changes to the configurations of PC workstations. Guarding against such changes can be a complex task, since browser software (in fact, most software) assumes that the user has complete access to all options and files. Patrons may make changes maliciously or mischievously, or they may inadvertently change settings.

Many hardware and software products are now available to help secure PC workstations. There are no simple solutions, however, and every action to secure a workstation may inconvenience users. For example, most libraries want to prevent users from changing the browser's display options, but preventing display option changes can present problems for users with some types of visual impairment, who may need to adjust the font size or colors, or eliminate distracting background images.

In the rapidly changing world of the Web, libraries need to devote a considerable amount of time to loading new

and updated software. New file formats are being introduced constantly, especially in the area of sound, graphics, video, and animation, requiring new software plug-ins.
There are also many languages represented on the World
Wide Web, with different encoding systems for handling
non-Roman text, requiring additional software for display.
Most of the needed software is free or very inexpensive,
and can be downloaded directly from the Web, but it still
requires time, planning, and coordination. It is much better to anticipate our patrons' needs and download needed
software to all workstations during off hours, than it is to
try to do it on the fly (when someone needs a tax form
but can't get it without Adobe Acrobat, or finds the Russian poem needed for class, but can't view it without
Cyrillic language software).

The question, of course, is whose responsibility is it to
maintain all of these workstations? The answer will vary
from library to library, with many libraries recognizing the
need to have added technical support staff. Whoever is responsible for doing the actual maintenance, however, the
reference librarians must be actively involved in observing the use of the workstations and making sure that security considerations or software limitations do not make
things unnecessarily difficult for our users.

Troubleshooting also becomes a responsibility for the
reference staff, who will inevitably find themselves in the
role of first responder, even if there are technical support
staff members to take over once it is determined that the
problem can't be fixed by reloading a page, closing down
and reopening the browser, or doing some other simple
trick.

## PRINTING

Printing raises another complex set of issues. Libraries may become more and more digital, but they are certainly not becoming paperless, as we see patrons going through reams of paper, printing articles, maps, pictures, charts, forms, and so forth. Workstations can have individual printers, or printers can be networked. Individual printers are costly, take up space, and increase the number of units that need to be maintained. Individual printers, however, have some important benefits in terms of simplicity. Networked printers add another layer of complexity for troubleshooting, not to mention the complications of having print jobs for different people going to a single unit.

Some libraries do not charge for printing, while others are finding it necessary to impose a charge for cost recovery. Charging patrons is not easy. Libraries utilize a variety of coin- and card-operated printing systems, systems where patrons need to pick up and pay for printouts from a service desk, and a variety of honor systems. One problem is that patrons never want to pay for blank sheets or printing mistakes, thus sometimes necessitating refunds and creating difficult interactions with patrons. Many librarians who use the honor system feel that, although they might take in less money than with other types of charge systems, the time they save in dealing with problems is worth the difference.

Many reference librarians are finding that the amount of time devoted to technical tasks is increasing steadily. The World Wide Web and the software needed to access it is becoming much more complex, and the number of workstations in many libraries is increasing; these two factors combined are stretching the resources of many reference departments. This is an area where reference librarians must be proactive within their own library systems, documenting the time devoted to these new tasks, and working with administrators to make appropriate staffing arrangements. With the World Wide Web, we have access to an incredible array of resources, often without purchase or subscription cost or shelving space. The hidden cost of electronic resources, however, is something that many reference librarians have learned by hard experience—it takes a lot of time and attention to keep it all accessible.

## CONFIDENTIALITY: NEW CONCERNS

Reference librarians have always been concerned about preserving the confidentiality of our patrons, but the move to electronic resources raises some new concerns.

To manage access to public workstations, many libraries have some kind of reservation or sign-in procedure which requires patrons to identify themselves. In some libraries, people sign themselves up for PC time on log sheets, which means that anyone can see at a glance who was using which workstation at what time, at least for the current day.

If this information is retained, it can be combined with other information and used to link a particular patron to whatever activity happened at the PC during a particular time period. This could be information from the PC itself, or from Netscape's history file or cache files, for example. Or the information could come from the server logs at remote sites. Enhanced server logs on Web sites include dated and time-stamped records of activity, including the IP address which uniquely identifies a workstation. Viewing a particular document, displaying a certain image, sending an e-mail message from a Web-based e-mail service, or posting something on a message board—all of these actions could be traced back to an individual library workstation. Clearly, there are major issues involving confidentiality and liability, and the advice of the library's attorney should be sought in dealing with this evolving area of the law.

### Problems for Shared Workstations

PCs were designed as *personal* computers, and the assumption that the PC belongs to a single user runs through the operating system, browser software, and even the design of Web sites. Libraries generally use security software of various kinds to block users from changing browser configurations, but there are a number of other sensitive areas on a public workstation that require careful management.

Cache files, for example, keep copies of all recently viewed documents and images. The browser constantly compares the date and time stamp of documents in the cache to the date and time stamps of remote files requested by the user, and uses the cache copies if they haven't been superceded. On your own desktop, this serves to speed up your browsing experience, greatly reducing the number of files that have to be transferred, assuming that you tend to go back to the same sites. On a shared workstation, where users are likely to have totally different interests and browse different sites, having a large cache file can actually slow down browsing. There may even be copies of illegal material, including pornographic images, in the cache files of a workstation. This is another area that raises both confidentiality and liability issues, and the library should investigate the legal ramifications of either retaining or destroying such files.

A number of other browser features that serve to help users get back to previously visited sites are a convenience on a personal workstation and a possible source of confusion on a public one, where the sites visited by previous patrons are either irrelevant or possibly disturbing. Browsers use history files to retain a list of recently visited sites, with date and time stamp. These files can be accessed directly as a list, and are also used to change the color of links to pages that have been visited recently. Drop-down location bars on Netscape retain a list of recently visited pages if the URL was entered in the location bar, and the current version of Netscape has an AutoComplete feature where it anticipates what URL you are typing based on recently visited sites. This is handy on your own PC, and rather creepy on a public workstation, where the PC may "guess" all sorts of strange sites, based on the interests of previous patrons.

Cookie files, where passwords and other identifying information can be stored by remote sites, present even more potential problems. Persistent cookies are stored by a remote site in a file on the PC, and then read by that site when the PC connects again. Persistent cookies are used to greet returning users and provide them with customized services, including linking them to a customer account which contains information such as their credit card numbers and past purchasing history. This presents obvious problems for shared workstations. You can disable cookies entirely in the browser preferences or make the cookie file read-only (so that cookies are only retained in memory during a single browser session, and not written to the hard drive). These measures ensure that as long as patrons exit Netscape at the end of their sessions, nobody else will be able to access their account information on other systems.

### Sources of Information

All of these potential problems, and other security issues, can be managed through the use of various set-up configurations and security software, but none of this is simple, and new versions of software and new developments on the Web bring new problems. Fortunately, new solutions are being developed as well, with many new products coming along that can often automate and replace security measures commonly used by libraries just a few years ago. An inexpensive, popular software product called Window Washer (*www.webroot.com/washer.htm*), for example, can automatically remove cache files, temporary files, cookies, location bar URLs, and the like, basically destroying all traces of activity by patrons using public workstations. This software does not, of course, destroy traces of activity that may be logged at remote sites.

There are several sites with useful information on public workstation security and confidentiality issues. One is Public Access Computer Security for Windows 95/98 (*www.infopeople.org/Security/*), a collection of resources developed by California's InfoPeople Project. Another is Securing Netscape in the Public Library (*northville.lib.mi. us/tech/netscape.html*), by Andrew Mutch, with some practical tips on common problems.

By far the best resource, however, is the e-mail group WEB4LIB (*sunsite.berkeley.edu/Web4Lib/*), where all aspects of providing public World Wide Web access are discussed, and various solutions are discussed and compared. This is the first place to turn for new developments, and the WEB4LIB participants are good at balancing security and technical issues with the professional goals of providing patrons with free and confidential access to information. WEB4LIB also maintains a Reference Center, with some of the most helpful past postings and links to often-cited resources, and searchable archives.

## ACCEPTABLE USE

Much has been written about the problems of pornography on the World Wide Web, and the intellectual freedom, legal, and social issues associated with offering graphical access in a public environment. Libraries generally respond to these concerns in some combination of three ways: through the use of filtering software, by the physical arrangement of workstations, or by formal or informal acceptable-use policies. None of these solutions is completely successful, and libraries continue to struggle to balance competing interests and different points of view on this controversial and much-publicized issue.

Allowing open access to graphic pornography on public workstations can have a negative effect on the library environment for other users, and may even create a hostile work environment for staff which could be considered a form of sexual harassment.

Limiting open access to the World Wide Web, however,

raises serious issues of intellectual freedom, and can cause practical issues as well. Professors have been known to assign research in pornographic Web sites to students in classes on human sexuality; students access extremely offensive material in researching topics such as hate crimes—librarians know that there isn't any subject that can't be the subject of serious research.

### Filtering Software

The use of filtering software may reduce the amount of graphic pornography that can be accessed by the workstation, but regardless of whether filters work on keyword or by screening out known pornographic sites, they will inevitably block some sites that should be acceptable and miss some that should be blocked (even if we could all agree on what constitutes "acceptable"). Filtering software varies in the amount of control the library can exercise in adjusting the configuration to the needs of the library. The use of filtering software can create a false sense of security for users, especially parents, who might assume that the software will be 100 percent effective—which it's not.

Libraries have tried two opposite methods of arranging workstations, in an attempt to manage the pornography problem. Some place workstations in very public areas, with screens easily visible to staff and other patrons, with the theory that this will shame users into keeping it clean. Undoubtedly, this does discourage many users from straying into the seamier areas of the Web, but there are others who enjoy being seen looking at these sites. Some librarians have reported being harassed by patrons who look at pornographic sites in front of them, ask for unnecessary help, and enjoy the librarians' discomfort. Arranging workstations so that they are very visible also denies all patrons any sense of privacy, whatever they are doing.

The opposite approach, of course, is to place workstations in such a way that screens are not visible to staff or passers-by, or to use privacy screens (which limit the view of the screen to someone directly in front of it) or computer tables in which the monitor is recessed beneath a clear surface. Such arrangements do provide some privacy, with the negative factor of making it more difficult for staff members to observe patrons who may be having a problem and need assistance.

### Policies

Libraries also may have acceptable use policies which patrons may be asked to sign before using Internet workstations. Some libraries display the library policy on a screen, so that patrons must click on a button that states they agree to abide by the policy in order to access the Internet. Typical acceptable use policies may refer not only to pornography, but also to any sort of illegal activity using the library's computer.

Informal policies include what have become known as "tap-on-the-shoulder" policies, in which the library does not use any filtering software but users are asked to close offensive sites if the staff notices them on the screen or other patrons complain. This method can be effective in maintaining control, but can result in encounters that are awkward for both staff and patrons.

## BEYOND REFERENCE

When the Internet first made its way into libraries, our presumption was that it was a "reference" thing. After all, it had to be used in the library so it didn't belong with the circulating collection, and patrons would need help with the workstations so it needed to be in a well-staffed area. We tended to think of Internet access the way we thought of other familiar computer resources, (like online services and CD-ROM products)—as a set of databases to be used for research.

And yet, the Internet has evolved into something quite different, and much more complex than that. People with home access to the Internet use it for a variety of purposes other than research—they play games, track stocks, read the news, shop for everything from airline tickets to groceries, gamble, apply for jobs, study for degrees, send baby pictures to relatives, keep in touch with friends, and chat with strangers. People who know that we offer World Wide Web access in the library often already have experience with all of this, expect to have full access to the Internet, and want to do more than just look at pages of information.

### *Chat and E-mail*

When the Internet first came to libraries, e-mail, USENET, and chat were generally not included services. They generally required accounts on a host system, and although some libraries did give patrons e-mail accounts, either independently or as part of a community Freenet, most did not.

Over the past few years, however, with the development

of the World Wide Web, things have changed. In 1996, HotMail, a free Web-based e-mail service was introduced, and it quickly became one of the most popular sites on the Web. Web-based mail services allow people to access their e-mail from any PC with a connection to the Internet, without any local configurations, e-mail programs, or dial-up numbers. Several other similar Web-based mail services followed. Web mail is a "sticky application"—it keeps users coming back to a site over and over, building the traffic that is important for generating advertising. Major search sites like Yahoo and Excite have added their own Web-based mail services, transforming themselves into "portals" or gateways to the World Wide Web.

Deja.com (*www.deja.com*) provides free, Web-based access to USENET newsgroups. Various Web-based forms of chat and discussion boards can be found on many sites. These forums can be general, ongoing discussion groups or special events like online interviews with writers, entertainers, and other well-known people.

This type of interpersonal communication is one of the important factors in the explosive growth of the Internet. In *The Virtual Community*, Howard Rheingold describes the development of computer-mediated communication (CMC) around the world and notes one recurring theme: big institutions tend to think of CMC in terms of a database, a way of distributing large sets of information to people "who spend their time interacting with information," but people themselves "almost always use CMC to communicate with each other in new ways unforeseen by the system's original designers. People everywhere seem more interested in communicating with each other than with databases" (Rheingold, 1993).

Some libraries, reasoning that their mission is to provide information, not to facilitate interpersonal communication, do not allow e-mail or chat on library workstations. A common analogy is that libraries do not provide telephones for making personal calls. As e-mail and chat become more tightly integrated into the rest of the Web, however, this becomes a more difficult policy to enforce. For example, many Web sites have mail-based Ask-an-Expert features, or they solicit comments and corrections by e-mail.

In fact, some important information resources operate almost entirely by e-mail. The Afrigeneas Database has a Surname Index (*members.aol.com/afriamgene/surnames/ search.html*), which allows users to search for an African-American surname and send an e-mail message to someone who is doing genealogical research on that family. Having access to e-mail allows our patrons to exchange information and participate in this kind of ongoing research, rather than making them wait and be the passive recipients of the information when it is eventually published.

It is difficult to enforce policies forbidding the use of e-mail or chat on public workstations unless librarians are actively checking screens to see what users are doing. It's also problematic to try to limit the use of the workstation not by the content of the material but by the format that content is presented in.

Academic libraries, which have a more defined role than public libraries, can run into complicated situations when, in an attempt to limit the use of their workstations to research, they prohibit students from accessing their e-mail in the library. Faculty members often communicate with

students by e-mail, students use e-mail to work cooperatively on group projects, and the library itself may send
notices about overdues or ILL requests by e-mail. Students
who can't check their e-mail in the library may find that
they have missed essential information that they needed
as part of their library visit.

As more reference resources move to electronic format,
and to the Web rather than CD-ROM stand-alone workstations, many academic institutions now have campus-
wide access to these library resources. Students who can't
access their e-mail in the library may find that they can
instead access all the same library resources in computer
labs, where they can also do e-mail; they may simply
choose to avoid using the more limited library workstations.

The public library perspective is, of course, different.
Public libraries have entertainment as part of their mission—they provide patrons with popular recreational reading material—and much of what people want to do on the
World Wide Web is more recreational than research oriented. This recreational use may be a somewhat uncomfortable fit when all Internet workstations are in reference,
a department that is generally quieter and more research
oriented than the rest of the library. Some libraries have
workstations both in reference and in other areas of the
building.

Many libraries have decided that they will not try to
limit either the content or the format of patrons' use of
the Internet, but instead they will impose some system of
time limit to ensure that everyone has access to the workstations. This approach keeps librarians out of the business of trying to decide who is doing something valuable

and who is just wasting time. Managing these time limits, however, can be time-consuming. Many libraries also allow patrons to reserve a block of time, which can add to the difficulties of managing access to workstations.

### Personalized Information Services

In addition to free, Web-based e-mail and USENET news, there is now a wide range of exciting, personalized services that our patrons can use. Many sites have a general set of resources, with special features available to anyone who signs up for a (usually free) account. For example, anyone can search for jobs at the Monster.com (*www.monster. com*), but by registering, users can post their resumes, or perform a search and have the Search Agent notify them by e-mail when new listings that meet the criteria become available.

Stock-tracking services are also popular. Instead of looking up individual stocks in the newspaper, users can set up an account, enter the stock symbols that they would like to track, and return to the site whenever they want to check on their stocks. In true Web fashion, stock-tracking sites make extensive use of hyperlinking to provide related information about each company, including company profiles, searches for recent news stories, SEC filings, and links to the company's own Web site. Many sites offer stock-tracking features, including the popular Motley Fool financial site (*www.fool.com*) and portal sites like Yahoo (*www.yahoo.com.*)

In fact, sites like Yahoo can do more than track stocks; they can also allow you to design your own customized information environment. With My Yahoo, you can design a personal start page that includes local weather reports, television and movie listings, sports, and daily horoscope, in any combination and in various arrangements on the page. You can also add Yahoo categories that you frequently visit, and customized news, choosing which categories of information to include. Configuring a site like this can take a little time and effort, but once it's done it can be a great convenience.

Many commercial sites offer customized services. Travel sites like Travelocity (*www.travelocity.com*) will remember your flight preferences, send you e-mail when fares go down to your favorite places, and even send a message to your alphanumeric pager about last-minute changes for any flight you booked through this service.

The ultimate in free Web-based services may be services like GeoCities (*www.geocities.com*) and Tripod (*www.tripod.com*), which allow you to design your own Web pages either by writing your own HTML or by filling out forms. The existence of such free services, combined with libraries offering free World Wide Web access, means that almost anyone can not only use the World Wide Web, but can become a part of it, without owning a computer or having any special training.

The World Wide Web is not a commercial service or collection of databases like LEXIS/NEXIS or FirstSearch. It's an interactive, hyperlinked, global collaborative effort. Libraries need to look at the services that are beyond the traditional scope of just searching/viewing/printing and decide whether these are services that they should limit, permit, or actively promote to their library users.

## REFERENCE AND LIBRARY WEB PAGES

In addition to being users of the World Wide Web, libraries are also actively involved in developing Web-based resources to be used by their own staff and patrons and by others around the world. Reference librarians are often active participants in this process, bringing their special perspective to the task.

One important role of any library Web site is to provide information about the library and its collections and services. Reference librarians should use the library's Web site to actively promote their services. It's good to tell people about reference services, but it's much better to *show* people, through the inclusion of guides and pathfinders, for example, and collections of past questions and answers.

The second role of a library Web site is to serve as a gateway to other library resources, including the library catalog, patron services (such as reserves, renewals, and checking on fines), and licensed databases. The gateway function can get complicated, since these resources often work differently within the library and remotely. For example, in a consortium or multibranch institution, the online catalog usually performs scoping and other local display options based on the location of the workstation. Remotely, the local functions may be determined based on the location information in the patron record, or by menu options, or the remote catalog may be a generic version, without scoping or other location-based functions. For licensed databases, validation is generally based on the IP addresses of workstations within the library, and remote use, if permitted, must be validated by patron barcode, student ID, or some similar system. In order to work around these gateway problems, it is often necessary to design slightly different versions of the Web site for in-library and remote use.

An optional role of the library Web site is to serve as a gateway to selected World Wide Web resources. This gateway can range from a few selected links for important local sites to a comprehensive World Wide Web directory that rivals Yahoo in size and complexity. Most libraries choose to do something in between, providing selected links to a representative sampling of high-quality, stable World Wide Web sites in high-interest subject areas.

Libraries face some interesting issues when selecting links for their Web pages. When we provide open access to the World Wide Web, we cannot take responsibility for the sites that people visit on our workstations. However, when we select links for our Web sites, we are in effect building a virtual collection, and are recommending the sites that we have chosen. Since World Wide Web sites may change location and content at any time, maintaining a collection of links is a time-consuming project, causing many libraries to choose not to attempt to provide a comprehensive collection. Instead they point users to some recommended directory sites and search engines, supplementing these external links with local links and special pages (like Staff Favorites or seasonal links).

In addition to the general directory and search sites like Yahoo (*www.yahoo.com*) and Lycos (*www.lycos.com*), there are some major projects of special value to libraries. Librarians' Index to the Internet (*sunsite.berkeley.edu/ InternetIndex/*) is a collection of links selected for their relevance to the needs of the public library user. This site began as the Gopher bookmark of Carole Leita, who still manages the project. In 1997 it was moved to a system at the University of California at Berkeley, where Leita worked with Roy Tennant to develop a sophisticated system of programming that allows a trained team of librarians around California to make additions and updates to the Index. The Index is well organized, with browsing and searching functionality, and is an excellent starting point for most public library users.

The University of California system also hosts an excellent virtual library designed for academic library users: Infomine, Scholarly Internet Resource Collections (*lib-www.ucr.edu*). Infomine is aimed at faculty, students, and research staff at the university level, and includes several different directories, including Government Information, Social Sciences & Humanities, and Visual & Performing Arts. Infomine is a project of the library of the University of California, Riverside, with participation from librarians at all nine University of California campuses and Stanford University, making it a good example of a distributed Internet resource collection project. Infomine uses Library of Congress subject headings, and the collection can be browsed or searched in a variety of ways.

## SPECIAL COLLECTIONS

Many libraries of all types and sizes have special collections, which may include books, recordings, pictures, maps, sound recordings, and other kinds of material. These collections may relate to local history or prominent people who lived in the community. Sometime libraries acquire

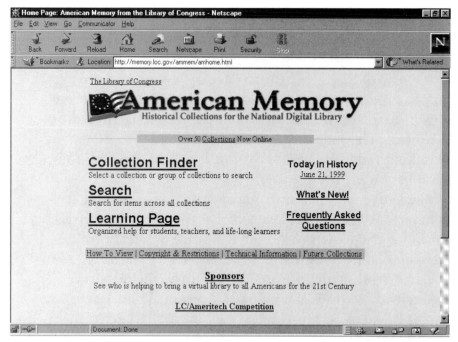

Figure 9–2. The American Memory Project at the Library of Congress.

special collections from local residents, and the subject of these can be just about anything.

The problem with these collections traditionally has been that their use was limited to those who knew about them and who were able to travel to the library. Books from special collections have sometimes been accessible through interlibrary loan, but other interesting and valuable material has often remained in the files for years between scholarly visitors.

Now libraries have an opportunity to make these collections available to anyone, anywhere, over the World Wide Web. This is a fine example of the move from reactive to proactive librarianship. The leader in this movement

**Figure 9–3. The Learning Page from the American Memory Project.**

is unquestionably the American Memory project of the Library of Congress (*memory.loc.gov/ammem/*). American Memory (Figure 9–2) consists of many collections, covering many aspects of American history, and in many formats, including photographs, maps, document images, text, sound recordings, and video. Collections include Selected Civil War Photographs, 1861–1865, Documents from the Continental Congress and the Constitutional Convention, 1774–1789, and By Popular Demand: Jackie Robinson and Other Baseball Highlights, 1860s-1960s.

The American Memory project continues to grow as new collections are added and existing collections are enriched. This is a model project not only in the wealth of material

## The World Wide Picture Show

Sometimes words aren't enough to describe a person, a place, an object, or an event. Photographs, maps, paintings, prints—many different types of visual material—can be found on the World Wide Web, giving even the smallest library an array of picture sources that none of us would have believed possible ten years ago. Here are some collections of pictures that must be seen to be believed!

The Thinker Art Imagebase
*www.thinker.org*

The Fine Arts Museum of San Francisco describes itself as "a public museum with an evolving mission to behave more like a resource and less like a repository," and a goal of making its complete collection available electronically. They are more than halfway there, with over 70,000 artworks of all types available as high-quality digital images, fully cataloged with excellent searching capabilities and interesting features like the ability to "zoom" images to different sizes. Many museums have excellent Web sites, but this one is really outstanding.

Selected Civil War Photographs
*memory.loc.gov/ammem/cwphome.html*

With over 1,100 photographs, this collection covers every aspect of the Civil War and includes portraits of Union and Confederate generals, battlefields, camp life, hospitals, and more. All photographs are meticulously documented and cataloged, with browsing and keyword searching ability. Several special features provide context to the collection, including a timeline that provides a chronological guide to major events of the War, with links to photographs, and special presentations on selected topics.

Teachers and students will appreciate the Learning Page, which provides search tips and links to related American Memory collections and other Web sites, and a fascinating feature called Does the Camera Ever Lie?, with examples of deceptive photographic practices by Civil War photographer Alexander Gardner.

NAIL: National Archival Information Locator
*www.nara.gov/nara/nail.html*

The National Archives and Records Administration (NARA) site features a number of interesting projects and exhibits, with lesson plans and other supporting material for educators. But the best thing they offer is NAIL, the prototype for an online catalog of the NARA collections. NAIL provides searchable access to 100 thousand digital copies (mostly graphics) from NARA centers around the nation including the presidential libraries.

This huge collection includes photographs on every aspect of World War II, from bond drives to Japanese internment camps; Lewis Hines's poignant photographs of child laborers; photographs of the presidents shaking hands with almost every well-known person of the 20th century; and much more—and it's all in the public domain.

Portrait Gallery
*www.lib.utexas.edu/Libs/PCL/portraits/portraits.html*

Need a picture of Kipling or Kepler in a hurry? The Perry-Castañeda Library, University of Texas at Austin, famous for its Historical Map Collection, has another simple but useful project: this gallery of public-domain portraits of well-known people. They are scanning the portraits from various reference books, old enough to be beyond copyright restrictions, and putting them here. No fancy index or searching capabilities, just an index by name, with a source listing for each portrait. This site is a tool, rather than an online exhibit, but it's a very handy tool for reference librarians.

The Amazing Picture Machine
*www.ncrtec.org/picture.htm*

The Amazing Picture Machine is not a search engine, but a searchable catalog of images selected from authoritative, stable Web sites. Each picture added to the catalog gets a brief description, some keywords, and a link, making the catalog easy to use and making it easy to pinpoint relevant hits.

This is a project of the North Central Regional Technology in Education Consortium, and reflects the needs of the K–12 school community. Coverage is best in areas frequently needed for school reports: presidents, national parks and monuments, architecture, the Civil War, animals, and dinosaurs, for example. You won't find everything you need, but it's so easy to use it's a good place to start for common picture requests.

that is being made available, but in the way that material is organized and presented. There are multiple ways to search or browse individual collections or across all collections. There's also a Learning Page (*lcweb2.loc.gov/ ammem/ndlpedu/*), which provides information especially helpful for teachers, students, and librarians on ways to use these collections in education (Figure 9–3). There are even special features for young students, including weekly jigsaw puzzles of images from the collection and Become a Historical Detective (*lcweb2.loc.gov/ammem/ndlpedu/ detectiv.html*), which teaches children historical research skills as they solve a mystery.

Another outstanding library special collection is the Perry-Castañeda Library Map Collection (*www.lib.utexas. edu/Libs/PCL/Map_collection/*) of the University of Texas at Austin with over 2,000 public-domain maps (Figure 9–4). The organization of the site is simple: the collection is divided into a few major divisions which may be divided into a few subdivisions and then the maps themselves are simply listed alphabetically. Descriptions include the source of the map and the size of the file.

Compared to the American Memory collections, which are designed almost as exhibits, this site is utilitarian in design. It has all the features that really matter, however. All of these maps are in the public domain, so users may freely download them for their own use. Since many of the maps are quite large, the FAQ file gives helpful information on using shareware graphics software to resize and print maps. The maps are also available by FTP, a helpful alternative with large files.

Most libraries do not have special collections that rival those of the Library of Congress, but most libraries have

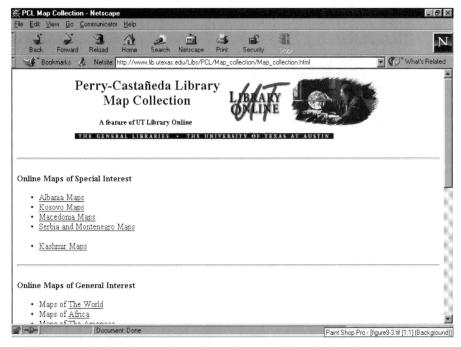

**Figure 9–4. The Perry-Castañeda Library Map Collection.**

some unusual and interesting photographs or other resources that could be digitized and made available over the World Wide Web. You can start small, with a few items, and gradually develop the online collection, adding new items and new features as time and resources allow. Many of the American Memory projects are based on popular demand, using past requests for reproductions as the basis of selection. Most libraries have a few requests that recur over the years: a photograph of the old train station that was torn down in the 1960s, newspaper accounts of a terrible fire, some historical local maps, and so on. Adding these items to your library Web site can be the beginning of developing an online special collection.

## THE WORLD WIDE WEB, TODAY AND BEYOND

The World Wide Web, quite simply, changes everything. It's the information superhighway, the information marketplace, the information playground, and more and more people of all ages are using the Web for everything from baseball scores to medical research. Reference librarians need to be a part of this brave new world, and we need to find new roles for ourselves in this greatly changed world of information. We need to provide access to the World Wide Web in our libraries, in ways that are fair to the needs of all users and as free of restrictions and limitations as possible. We need to provide help, online and off, to guide our users through the maze of available information. We need to make our own resources available online, including the catalog, patron services, licensed databases, pathfinders, booklists, and special collections.

Libraries can also benefit from studying the way that major Web sites, not bound by bureaucracy or tradition, are constantly changing and adding new features to keep the attention of their users. The World Wide Web is constantly evolving, becoming larger, richer, more complex, more personalized, more useful, and more entertaining. Our libraries need to evolve in all the same ways, or we risk being left behind.

## LOOKING AHEAD: FIVE TRENDS THAT WILL AFFECT REFERENCE SERVICES

Predicting the future is always a risky business, and on the World Wide Web change happens quickly. However, certain trends seem likely to continue that will affect all libraries.

1. Almost everyone will be there.

   This one seems certain. More and more people go online every day, and connection to the Internet will soon reach the saturation point (like the telephone, radio, and television)—almost everyone will be connected, except for those who are truly poor or who decide not to participate. The cost of access keeps falling, along with the cost of computers. WebTV and similar devices make it even easier for people who are resistant to computers to be a part of the World Wide Web. Online services no longer cater to the technological elite, but to beginners. The more people who are on the Web, the easier it is for nervous newbies to come aboard, since they can easily find friends and family members to assist them, and books, magazines, and classes aimed at newcomers are easy to find.

   Libraries will find that as more people have access elsewhere, there will be less demand for public workstations. Library workstations will be used less often by total novices, and more by people who are temporarily without access, or who are in the library to use other materials or to work with a reference librarian. Libraries will be able to divert some of the time and energy currently dedicated to the logistics of managing the high demand for public workstations; instead they will develop workshops and guides on World Wide Web resources.

2. Seach tools will continue to improve.
World Wide Web search sites are constantly improving. Search engines are using more sophisticated algorithms to improve relevance, and are exploring improved ways to present results to users. For example, many sites now use some sort of post-search processing to cluster results or to suggest additional search terms to increase relevance. Other areas of intense development are specialized search engines for different types of media (especially images and sounds) or different subject areas. Meta search engines, which send a search to many different search engines and combine the search results, are also improving.

This means that our library patrons will spend less time hopelessly lost in the Web, and they will be able to find material related to their topic of interest. Librarians will spend less time helping people get started and more time helping them evaluate the material they have found. We can also help our users learn how to use the more advanced and specialized features of search engines. In addition, we can help them find all the specialized databases and other resources not accessible on the Web.

3. It will be a multimedia world.
Multimedia of all types will continue to develop on the World Wide Web. Graphics are well established, and now sound and video technology is improving

rapidly. As the quality improves, more sites offer substantial content in these formats, stimulating further development. Shockwave, Flash, and other technologies that promote interactivity are increasingly important. Another trend is the interaction between PC browsers and various small, portable devices, such as MP3 audio players, digital cameras, and handheld PCs.

Libraries will need to respond to these developments by continuing to upgrade workstations, browsers, and plug-ins, and to find ways to provide sound (through speakers, headphones, or other means). We will also need to prepare for a public that increasingly regards library workstations as they would a college computer lab, (and thus they expect to be able to download songs to their digital sound players, upload pictures from their digital camera to their Web-based e-mail accounts, and synchronize their PalmPilots and Yahoo calendars).

4. User diversity will require creative planning.
The World Wide Web is not just for the young, affluent, and technologically savvy. We are now seeing a much wider cross section of the community, more diverse in terms of age, language, economic status, and special needs.

Fortunately, the technology is flexible and adaptable, although sometimes it's difficult to provide options on shared, public workstations. For our workstations to serve the needs of all our users, we will need to update language software as needed, and to attend to ergonomic concerns. Some users with vision problems may want to change font sizes, change colors, or turn off background images—simple changes that can make a big difference for many people. Left-handed people have difficulties with a right-handed mouse, and many people have difficulty handling a mouse at all. Users with carpal tunnel syndrome, arthritis, or other problems affecting manual dexterity would benefit from voice recognition software. Those with a high level of visual impairment also need text-reading software and Braille printers.

5. Shopping, talking, and learning will continue to evolve.

Using the World Wide Web goes beyond just searching for information and looking at the results. Library users, like others on the Web, can do much more: make travel reservations, go shopping or participate in online auctions, apply for jobs, pay parking tickets, participate in book discussion groups with people from around the world, or even run their own Web sites.

Many libraries have policies governing Internet access, which place limits on how patrons use our workstations. Many libraries prohibit the use of chat and e-mail. However, as Web services become more complex, so do the policy issues. If the policy prohibits e-mail and chat, can a patron post questions to a message board forum on a Web site? What about posting to USENET newsgroups through Deja.com? If the policy states that workstations are to be used for "information and research only," does that mean a user can't shop online? Where do the free Web site services fall under such a policy—can the user be an information provider, or just an information consumer? Many libraries are now devising policies that impose time limits rather than other types of restrictions on the use of public workstations.

Who knows what's next? New ideas come along on the Web all the time, and a few innovative sites have had profound influences. HotMail pioneered the concept of free Web-based e-mail, GeoCities popularized the idea of free Web sites, and eBay became an overnight sensation with its online auction site. As the World Wide Web continues to evolve, the only reliable prediction is that things will keep changing.

# Appendix A

# Sample Reference Policy

Libraries of all sizes and types benefit from having a written reference policy that sets basic standards and practices for the department. Such a document can be used for training new staff members, as a resource for all staff members when they encounter various situations, and for purposes of supervision and evaluation of department members.

The sample reference policy from North Suburban Library System (Wheeling, Ill.), which appears here, is particularly useful because it includes specific, practical guidelines. Many of the topics that come up repeatedly for discussion on LIBREF-L are covered, including homework help, contest questions, criss-cross including "near-bys," and personal recommendations.

Libraries may disagree on the best method of handling such questions, but whatever the library's policy on a particular matter is, it's more likely to be followed if it is written down, discussed with all staff members, and used for training and evaluation. The fact that librarians have so much disagreement on how to handle some of these issues is all the more reason for writing them down and discussing them in training—this helps avoid the situation where a librarian, following the practice at his former library, discovers that he has violated the policy of his new library only after the fact.

Reference policies should be reviewed by the reference staff and administration on a regular basis, perhaps annually, to keep everyone in touch with the policy, and to provide an opportunity to reconsider and amend guidelines as needed. Policies and guidelines regarding the use of public Internet workstations are not included in the sample document, written in 1992, but they should also be written and reviewed regularly.

## Reference Policy

### Introduction

The Policy Subcommittee, consisting of experienced reference librarians, many of whom are reference department managers, placed major emphasis on offering a practical document—one that not only contained statements of policy, but also guidelines for implementing policy. Although no document can prepare staff for every contingency, the subcommittee attempted to identify and address the primary issues confronting the reference staff member. These guidelines were arrived at through much spirited discussion. While members of the subcommittee agree that there are many alternatives to the suggested guidelines, there was unanimous agreement that each library, no matter its size, type, location and staffing policies, should address the identified issues in some manner and have a written document, consistently applied, upon which reference staff, professional or nonprofessional, can rely.

NSLS Reference Librarians Association Reference Policy Committee

Jan Baaske
*Indian Trails Public Library District*
Nancy Bodner
*Arlington Heights Memorial Library*
Eugenia Bryant
*Morton Grove Public Library*
Debby Grodinsky
*NSLS System Reference Service*
Kenneth Gross
*Northbrook Public Library*
Tom Kern
*Skokie Public Library*
Eileen Kloberdanz
*Cook Memorial Library*
Karen Maki
*Gail Borden Public Library District*
Jan Watkins
*Schaumburg Township District Library*

Joan Wilts
*Waukegan Public Library*

Elaine Burke, Chair
*Indian Trails Public Library District*

**NSLS Reference Policy Committee**
**Model Reference Guidelines**

**I.   Statement of Library's Mission**

The Library's primary mission is to provide materials and services to meet the informational, cultural and recreational needs of every resident of the community.

**II.  Mission of Reference Department**

It is the mission of the Reference Department to effectively meet these needs by bringing the library's resources and potential users together through a variety of services. Reference service will be provided at all times that the library is open. The reference desk will be staffed by the appropriate number of professionally trained staff necessary to provide quality service.

**III. Purpose of Reference Guidelines**

   1.  To describe the services and resources which are offered by the department.
   2.  To set standards and guidelines for service.
   3.  To provide guidance for those working at the reference desk and those being trained.

**IV. Reference Staff**

Reference staff members, whether professional or paraprofessional, serve as the link between library resources and the patron. As such, it is important that the staff member be:

   1.  Knowledgeable about library materials and services.
   2.  Open and approachable; friendly but professional.
   3.  Able to communicate effectively with people.
   4.  Discreet in the handling of questions which might be confidential or sensitive.
   5.  Able to exercise good judgment both in the interpretation of policy and in the handling of exceptional situations.

New staff members will receive orientation to the department, the library as a whole and the North Suburban Library System. On-going training is necessary in order to provide the highest level of service. Therefore, participation in library activities ranging from formal classroom instruction to informal groups sharing professional ideas is encouraged as is membership and participation in the Illinois Library Association and the American Library Association.

## V. Library Users

Reference service is available to all persons served by the Library regardless of age, sex, religion, race, social or economic status, or home library.

## VI. General Guidelines for Desk Service

### A. Priorities

Service to the public receives priority over any other duties. Clerical tasks, conversations with co-workers and other professional assignments are secondary. In-person and telephone requests for service should be handled in order of their arrival. If it becomes necessary to leave the desk for any length of time, another staff member should be informed and suitable arrangements made.

Although the Library's primary responsibility is to patrons within its district, there should be no discrimination against other patrons for basic reference service.

### B. Recording Statistics and Questions

Accurate statistics regarding service to patrons should be recorded. The methods used to gather statistics may be based on *Output Measures for Public Libraries*, 2nd. ed. Staff is urged to note the subject matter of questions of a difficult or unusual nature and indicate areas where more material is needed.

### C. Reporting Problems

If a staff member has a problem in dealing with a patron, the name and telephone number of the patron should be taken and given to the supervisor who will take appropriate action.

D.  Incomplete Reference Transactions

Questions that remain unanswered at the end of a staff member's desk shift may be passed on to incoming staff. Staff members are encouraged to consult with colleagues if they need help with a puzzling or difficult question. If the requested information cannot be provided within 24 hours, the patron should be notified of the status of the request.

E.  Referrals to North Suburban Library System Services

If the question cannot be answered in-house, it may be referred to the appropriate system service. The North Suburban Library System provides access to materials (books, periodicals, and A-V) and services (reference and continuing education) outside of an individual library's collection in order to provide a larger pool of resources. These resources are available through the following system services: Interlibrary Loan (ILL), Center Serials Services (CSS), System Reference Service (SRS), and Suburban Audio-Visual Services (SAVS).

F.  Referrals to Other Agencies

Referrals to other agencies may be made when appropriate. Patrons should be advised that they may contact the library for further assistance if they are not successful in obtaining help from the agency. At no time may staff refer the patron to individual practitioners—physicians, attorneys, mental health professionals, etc.

G.  Referrals to Other Libraries

If the staff member feels that it is appropriate to refer the patron to another library, it is important to verify that the material needed is actually there.

H.  Sources

To give the most accurate and authoritative answers possible, staff members should avoid personal opinions, philosophy, or evaluations; rather they should rely upon information obtained from reputable sources. The source of the answer should always be cited.

I.   Instruction and Orientation Services

Instruction and orientation services in library use are an integral part of library service and may range from basic instruction on how to use catalogs and reference tools to more formal assistance such as tours designed to increase the patron's knowledge of the library materials and services.

J.   Time Limits

In general, fifteen minutes should be the maximum amount of time to work with a patron. However, when the staff member has time available, additional time may be devoted to the question.

## VII. Specific Desk Guidelines

A.   In-Person Reference

1. Basic assistance—Never assume that a patron knows how to locate library materials. Assistance should be offered whenever a patron appears to need it. This may require accompanying the patron to the catalog to explain how to use it or accompanying the patron to the indicated area. Whenever patrons are sent to the stacks on their own, it is important to remind them to report back to the reference desk if they are unsuccessful in finding what they need.

2. Priority—If several people are waiting for assistance, requests that are either brief or that involve patron participation with staff guidance may be given priority over lengthy or complex questions that require large amounts of time. If a patron has a time-consuming request which is delaying service to other patrons, the staff member should offer to complete the question at a later time.

It may be necessary to work with several people at once—getting each started and then returning to make sure they are finding their information. Additional staff should be summoned if necessary.

B.   Telephone Reference

Telephone reference service should be used for short, factual information questions which do not require extensive reading or interpretation on the part of staff members. If the answer to a telephone question seems too involved to relate easily over the telephone, this should be explained to the patron and the suggestion made that the patron come to the Library. Staff will answer the telephone with a department name, such as Reference Desk, Information Desk or Young People's Services. If callers must wait, they should be given the option to remain on hold or to have their calls returned (get phone #). The staff member must call back as soon as possible. For calls from out-of-state, the callers should be asked to call back at a prearranged time.

When a staff member must transfer a call to another department, the caller should be told where the call is being transferred and why. The staff member transferring a call should convey to the other department the patron's question and what sources have been checked.

C.  Fax/Mail Reference

It is the Library's practice to respond to all reasonable reference inquiries by mail, fax or electronic bulletin board. The Department Head has the responsibility to refer the question to the appropriate staff member.

**VIII.  Specific Question Guidelines**

A.  School Assignments

Homework is intended to be a learning experience for the student. The role of the reference staff member is one of guidance in helping the student find the material or potential source of information to complete the homework assignment.

Every effort should be made to satisfactorily answer the student's question and provide the sources for information and the instruction needed to use those sources. However, the student is expected to use that material in order to meet the requirements of the assignment. The Reference staff member should not "write" the paper for the student or organize the information into the exact configuration needed to fulfill the assignment. Requests involving extensive research for homework projects will not be answered by telephone.

If every effort has been made by the Reference staff member and the student to locate information without results, the student will be encouraged to return to the teacher for further instructions or an altered assignment. A note to this effect may be given the student if the Reference staff member feels it is justified.

B. Contest Questions

Simple, factual contest questions should be treated in the same manner as all other reference questions. Some contest questions are tricky and might have more than one answer which seems to be correct. The Library does not guarantee that the answer provided is the correct answer for any particular contest. The staff should not conduct lengthy searches, interpret contest rules or do work which should be done by patrons.

C. Consumer Evaluations

The staff should help patrons locate objective consumer product information by showing them how to consult the indexes to *Consumer Reports* and related magazines, buying guides, and/or general indexes which may lead to product evaluations in other periodicals. The staff should not offer personal opinions recommending one product or another.

D. Book, Antique and Art Appraisals

Patrons may be referred to appropriate reference sources or to consultants or experts. Staff members should never give a personal appraisal regarding the monetary value of a patron's possession.

E. Critical Analyses of Literary Works

Staff members should not provide personal critical analyses, interpretations, or judgments regarding the merit of literary or other works (including the patron's own writing efforts).

F. Genealogical Questions

Staff members should provide general assistance in genealogical research, guidance in locating items in the collection, and help in obtaining resources through Interlibrary Loan, but should not engage in actual genealogical research for patrons.

G.  Translations

Translations should be provided only if a person on the staff with appropriate expertise is available. Otherwise, staff should contact System Reference Service or other appropriate resources to obtain information regarding translators.

H.  Compilations and Extensive Research

Patrons needing extensive compilations or research (bibliographies, lists, statistics, etc.) should be directed to the appropriate resources and offered as much assistance as staff time allows.

I.  Mathemical Calculations

Staff members should not perform mathematical calculations for patrons. Information from tables and formulas may be consulted, or an electronic calculator may be provided, but patrons should do their own calculations.

J.  Medical and Legal Questions

The Library does not provide advice in the areas of medicine and law. If legal information can be found in printed sources, it is provided. However, complicated legal searches should not be undertaken nor should personal interpretations of legal matters be offered. In regard to telephone requests for medical information, brief definitions and descriptions from authoritative published sources may be provided. These sources should be quoted verbatim with no personal interpretation. The patron should be informed of the source from which the information is taken. Under no circumstances should staff offer advice in these areas, regardless of how commonplace the knowledge seems to be. If more information is required, the patron should be encouraged to examine the Library's collection or be referred to another source.

K.  Criss-Cross and City Directories

Criss-cross or city directory inquiries will be answered by telephone or in person. No more than three listings will be provided per patron at any one time. A maximum of two "nearby's" per listing will be provided. (Some libraries may wish to rule out "nearby's" altogether for telephone requests).

L.   Taxation Questions

Staff members should not provide advice in the interpretation of tax law or assistance in the selection of appropriate forms.

## IX.  Online Searching

Online searching may be done at the discretion of the staff member in order to save time and/or in order to provide more complete or more current information. The staff member's judgment will prevail in determining whether or not this is the most appropriate resource to use.

If the cost of the search exceeds $_____, the patron must pay the balance. This should be agreed upon prior to the execution of the search.

Time frame: online search requests should be handled using the same guidelines as any other reference request.

(Some libraries may wish to include the following restrictions, provided here simply as examples:

If residency requirements are a factor, include:
Patron must be a library card holder.

If searches are limited to a specific number per time period, include:
Each patron is entitled to one online search regarding a single topic per month.)

## X.   Loan of Reference Materials [Optional]

With the approval of the staff member on duty at the reference desk, reference material may be signed out from the Library for time periods during which the library is closed. The staff member should determine that a circulating copy is not available and that the patron's borrowing record is clear.

The loan period should be as brief as possible—overnight to three days. Longer periods must be approved by the head of the department. Exceptions to this policy may be made for the following materials which may be signed out more liberally, but for no more than one week:

Earlier editions of reference materials
Specialized collections
Books containing slides, such as art books

Examples of materials that may never be signed out from the Library include:

| | |
|---|---|
| Ready-reference materials | Book or periodical indexes |
| Closed reference materials | Expensive materials |
| Frequently used materials | Materials from multi-volume sets |

No more than three reference items per patron may be signed out at the same time.

The fine for an overdue reference item is $ _____ per (day or hour), up to the cost of the item plus the fee for processing the item's replacement.

Because of an unlimited variety of circumstances which may enter into requests for loans, each loan request should be treated as a new situation.

# Appendix B

# Sample Survey Form

The use of patron questionnaires is one way to gather information for the evaluation of reference service. Survey forms should be given to all patrons during designated weeks, in order to evaluate reference service as a whole and not just during "prime time." It's helpful to date and time-stamp forms, or otherwise designate days of the week and shift changes in order to identify times when reference service is significantly strong or weak.

The following sample form was developed by the North Suburban Library System. The first several questions ask about some very specific staff behaviors. The last two questions, asking patrons if they liked the way the librarians served them and if they would return to the same librarian for help in the future, are much more subjective, but are the ultimate measures of success from the patron's point of view. Patrons are encouraged to add comments, which can provide context for interpreting the answers to the questions.

## How Are We Doing?

*Please let us know how we can serve you better!*

If you asked any of the librarians for help today, please answer the questions below. You can use the space at the bottom and/or on the reverse side of the page for any other comments or ideas.

|  | Yes | No | Don't Know | Not Appl. |
|---|---|---|---|---|
| 1. Was the librarian easy to find? |  |  |  |  |
| 2. Did the librarian greet you and offer to help you? |  |  |  |  |
| 3. If the librarian was helping another person, did he/she offer to help you as soon as possible? |  |  |  |  |
| 4. Did the librarian seem interested in your question? |  |  |  |  |
| 5. Did the librarian talk with you to be *sure* of your needs? |  |  |  |  |
| 6. a.) Did you get the information you needed? <br> b.) If not, did the librarian tell you where you could get it? |  |  |  |  |
| 7. a.) Did the librarian help you find the information you needed? <br> b.) Did you get enough help and explanation? |  |  |  |  |
| 8. Did the librarian ask you if you had found what you needed and encourage you to come back for more help? |  |  |  |  |
| 9. Did you like the way the librarian assisted you? |  |  |  |  |
| 10. Would you want to ask the same librarian for help in the future? |  |  |  |  |

Comments:

# Sources Cited

Adler, Mortimer. 1983. *How to Speak, How to Listen.* New York: Macmillan.

Clark, Juleigh Clark and Karen Cary. 1995. "An Approach to the Evaluation of Ready Reference Collections." *RSR* (Spring): 39–43. MasterFile Premier. Online. EBSCO Publishing <AN: 9509144644>. 29 July 1999.

Eastman, L. A. 1897. "Aims and Personal Attitude in Library Work." *Library Journal* 22, no. 10, 80–81

Green, Samuel Swett. 1876. "Personal Relations Between Librarians and Readers." *Library Journal* 1, nos. 2–3, 74–81.

Holmes, Susan F. 1998. "Reaching the Whole Community through the Internet." *Computers in Libraries,* 18, no. 4: 51–55. MasterFile Premier. Online. EBSCO Publishing <AN: 448307>. 29 July 1999.

Isenstein, Laura. 1992. "Get Your Reference Staff on the STAR Track." *Library Journal* 117, no. 7, 34–37.

Kay, Alan S. 1997. "Banking on the Net." *Communications Week,* no. 570 (August 14): 35–39.

Lankes, R. David. 1999. "Building the Virtual Reference Desk." Syracuse: ERIC Clearinghouse for Information & Technology. Online. *www.vrd.org/TelEd.html.* 29 July 1999.

———. 1998. "Information Mentoring: Guidelines for Providing Reference Service to K-12." Syracuse: ERIC Clearinghouse for Information & Technology. Online. *www.vrd.org/training/training.html* 22 October 1998.

*Library Journal* (Editorial staff). 1996. "Historical Highlights from the

Pages of *LJ*." *Library Journal* 121, no. 12: 57–69. MasterFile Premier. Online. EBSCO Publishing <AN: 9607307603>. 29 July 1999.

Majka, David R. 1995. "An Electronic Tickler File for Reference Collection Management." *Library Software Review* 14, no. 3, (Fall): 146–153.

McDermott, Irene E. 1998. "Virtual Reference for a Real Public." *Searcher* 6, no. 4, (April): 25–31.

McMorran, Charles. 1997. "Walking the Multilingual Walk." *American Libraries* 28, no. 10, 46.

Morgan, Linda. 1980. "Patron Preferences in Reference Service Points." *RQ*, 19 (Summer): 373–375.

North Suburban Library Association. Reference Librarians Association. 1992. "Reference Evaluation Project." Wheeling, Ill. : Reference Librarians Association, North Suburban Library System.

Pierson, Robert. 1977. "On Reference Desks." *RQ* 17 (Winter): 137–138.

Relmen, A.S., 1983. "Lessons from the Darsee Affair." *New England Journal of Medicine* 308, (June 9): 1415–1417.

Rheingold, Howard. 1993. "The Virtual Community: Homesteading on the Electronic Frontier." Reading, Mass.: Addison-Wesley.

Ryan, Hank Phillippi. 1998. "Hank Phillippi Ryan Investigates—Who Ya Gonna Call?" Broadcast. WHDH-TV (February 9).

Sarkodie-Mensah, Kwasi. 1992. "Dealing with International Students in a Multicultural Era," *Journal of Academic Librarianship*, 18 no. 4, 214–217. MasterFile Premier. Online. EBSCO Publishing <AN: 9705210004>. 29 July 1999.

Stalker, John C. and Marjorie E. Murfin. 1996. "Quality Reference Service: A Preliminary Case Study." *Journal of Academic Librarianship*, 22, no. 6 (November): 423–428. MasterFile Premier. Online. EBSCO Publishing <AN: 9701173480>. 29 July 1999.

Stasek, Mary Ellen. 1998. Personal e-mail correspondence with author.

Tate, Marsha and Jan Alexander. 1996. "Teaching Critical Evaluation Skills for World Wide Web Resources." *Computers in Libraries* 16, no. 10 (November/December): 49–54.

Tygett, Mary, V., Lonnie Lawson and Kathleen Weessies. 1996 " Using Undergraduate Marketing Students in an Unobtrusive Reference Evaluation." *RQ* 36, no. 2 (Winter 1996): 270–276.

Vogl, A.J. 1997. "Growing Pains." *Across the Board* 34, no. 2, (February) 43–48. MasterFile Premier. Online. EBSCO Publishing <AN: 9707194471>. 29 July 1999.

West, Sharon M. and Steven L. Smith. 1995. "Library and Computing Merger: Clash of the Titans or Golden Opportunity." Online. *www.educause.edu/ir/library/text/cnc9564.txt* 29 July 1999.

Wilhemus, David W. 1996. "Perspectives on Americans with Disabilities Act: Accessibility of Academic Libraries to Visually Impaired Patrons." *Journal of Academic Librarianship* 22, no. 5 (September/October): 366–370. MasterFile Premier. Online. EBSCO Publishing <AN: 9611060083>. 29 July 1999.

Wurman, Richard Saul. 1990. *Information Anxiety: What to Do When Information Doesn't Tell You What You Need to Know.* New York: Bantam Books.

York, Maurice C., 1997. "Value-Added Reference Service: The North Carolina Periodicals Index." *Computers in Libraries* 17, no. 5, (May): 30–33. MasterFile Premier. Online. EBSCO Publishing <AN: 9705143139>. 29 July 1999.

# Index

# About the Author

Elizabeth Thomsen is the member services manager for NOBLE, the North of Boston Library Exchange, a multitype library consortium. Her responsibilities at NOBLE include training and Web development. She is also a partner in Library Management Associates, specializing in library technology planning, staff training, and library building programs.

Thomsen is the Internet columnist for the journal *Collection Building* and author of *Reference and Collection Development on the Internet: A How-To-Do-It Manual for Librarians* (Neal-Schuman, 1996). She is known for her presentations on Internet-related topics at American Library Association, state, and regional conferences. Before coming to NOBLE, she worked for public libraries in Salem, Hamilton, Revere, and Wakefield, Massachusetts.